semi-gloss

MAGAZINES, MOTHERHOOD
AND MISADVENTURES IN HAVING IT ALL

JUSTINE CULLEN

ALLEN&UNWIN
SYDNEY • MELBOURNE • AUCKLAND • LONDON

First published in 2021

Copyright © Justine Cullen 2021

Allen & Unwin
83 Alexander Street
Crows Nest NSW 2065
Australia
Phone: (61 2) 8425 0100
Email: info@allenandunwin.com
Web: www.allenandunwin.com

 A catalogue record for this book is available from the National Library of Australia

ISBN 978 1 76087 535 0

Set in 12.5/18.5 pt Adobe Garamond Pro by Bookhouse, Sydney
Printed and bound in Australia by Griffin Press, part of Ovato

10 9 8 7 6 5 4 3 2 1

 The paper in this book is FSC® certified. FSC® promotes environmentally responsible, socially beneficial and economically viable management of the world's forests.

To H—all paths led to you

contents

Preface

BEHIND THE GLOSS

THIS BOOK IS not the Australian version of *The Devil Wears Prada*, aka *The Devil Wears Zimmermann*. It's not even *The Devil Wears Spanx and a Comfortable Low Heel*, as disappointingly accurate as that may be these days. This is no exposé of the world of glossy magazines, and there are no villainous Miranda Priestlys within its pages. That might be a let-down for anyone picking it up after recognising my name from some mildly amusing but mostly self-indulgent editor's letter in the front of a magazine they once read at the hairdresser's. If that's you, I'm so sorry. May I recommend *The Vanity Fair Diaries* by Tina Brown? It's really good.

This book is no self-help tome filled with millennial-friendly, Etsy-poster-worthy advice on life and love for young women, especially not on love—unless it's in the form of What Not To Do. I'm in my forties, you see, and your forties is the decade when you finally realise beyond all doubt that all you know for

sure is that you know literally nothing at all, which makes it a terrible time to write a book that people might read looking for some kind of guidance. If there are any Top Tips! at all to be garnered from these pages, I can't promise that they're anything more substantial than how to train your bladder to need to go to the bathroom less often on a deadline or perhaps how to drop your children off to daycare when they clearly have pinkeye and get away with it, so do with that what you will and godspeed.

This book is not a memoir. Are you even kidding me? I haven't done anything nearly interesting or important enough to write a memoir. It is a collection of thoughts, musings, random ponderings, reflections and unreliably recalled moments—a half-time scoreboard check, undertaken at that point in a life where things like youth, freedom, ambition and forward-facing nipples are close enough to feel like they were yesterday even as we stare middle age squarely in its saggy-jawed face and wonder how much longer we can possibly be expected to stay upright. Because that's how it happens. Your twenties go by so slowly—you feel it's the only age you'll ever be, like it's the only age that matters to anyone (especially when, like me, you work in an industry as anti-ageing as fashion). Then you turn thirty and time blurs to the point that sometimes you can lose entire years, like the life version of the kids' counting cheat, '1, 2, skip a few, 99, 100'. That's how I've felt about all my birthdays since around thirty-three. The very idea of 'middle age' is a myth because there is no middle ground when it comes to ageing. There's just Forever Young and then God, How Am I This Old.

This book is not my opus. Like every good mag hack, I'd always dreamt of the day I'd sit down to be a Proper Writer and write a Great Book—an act that, of course, would entail being holed up alone in a turreted room in an old house, sitting at a wooden desk in front of a small window overlooking rolling green hills, accompanied only by a warm and silently encouraging elderly aunt with nothing to do but plump my seat cushions and bring me cups of steaming cocoa as I type in a fury of inspired creativity.

What I've now worked out, though, is that to be a Proper Writer is something best attempted with the energy and idleness of youth on your side, and unfortunately by the time I'd stopped being super busy dating the wrong guys, rewatching old seasons of *The Bachelorette* and googling whatever happened to Jonathan Taylor Thomas, my youth and its corresponding energy and idleness was all used up. Also, in a practical sense, I have no such aunt, no such hills and more than that, as a mother, *I have no such alone.*

When I first agreed to write this book, I'd just quit my job as editor-in-chief of *Elle* magazine. It was the only job I'd ever wanted or expected to have in my life, right up until the day I realised that it wasn't. In the aftermath of my departure, rather than celebrating my new-found freedom by day-drinking pina coladas as I'd always pictured, I instead found myself suffering from a full-blown case of publishing PTSD. It caught me by surprise. I'd thought I was made of hardier stuff, but post-resignation I quickly realised that my identity and sense of self-worth were more tangled up with my fancy job title and an association with

a famous international magazine masthead than I'd known. The giveaway was that every time someone asked me what I did for a living, I'd feel a rising dread and find myself starting with, 'Well, I used to be the editor-in-chief of *Elle* magazine, but . . .'—a strange and awkward way to introduce yourself when you have a perfectly acceptable and interesting new job that you do now. And also I'd cry every time I accidentally wandered into the magazine aisle of Woolies, which was a pretty clear sign that I had some unresolved issues. I suppose it was understandable. My whole life I'd dreamt of being the editor-in-chief of *Elle*. Against all odds, I'd gone and become her. Once that part of me was gone, I couldn't help but grieve. I'd liked her. She'd always had excellent shoes.

In the meantime, I'd started my new job, which was something I never expected to have to do until it came time to retire to the Byron Bay hinterland to launch an artisanal cordial business. The new job was at a different company and in a different building to the storied 54 Park Street where I'd worked on *Dolly*, *Shop Til You Drop* and *Elle* magazines for fifteen years of my life—longer than any relationship I'd ever had or any address I'd ever called home. It was also in a completely different part of the industry and my first experience—since Ashton Kutcher convinced us that Twitter was a worthwhile way to spend our time—of having to genuinely learn things that were completely new to me. I was well and truly out of my comfort zone, and despite the advice typographic Pinterest quotes will give you about no great things ever coming from within comfort zones, at least mine had come with gifted Gucci handbags. So at the unsexy

and hitherto unimaginable age of forty-one, I found myself in the midst of something of an identity crisis. Did I mention I was pregnant with my fourth child? This was not the idyllic book-writing experience I'd imagined for myself.

Instead of the turret, I wrote on airplanes and in hotel rooms on work trips with jet lag. I wrote in bed with my laptop balancing on my belly while battling pregnancy insomnia. And on the toilet with my laptop balancing on my lap battling pregnancy constipation. I wrote in a corner of my living room trying to block out the sounds of my eldest son teaching himself the guitar by playing the first few bars of Nirvana's 'School' over and over and over (and over and over) again. I wrote whenever I could bribe my other children with more screen time just to get a little bit of blessed silence. At one point I tried dictating into my phone on my daily commute, but found myself going off on so many tangents I started to fear conversation in case that's what talking to me was actually like IRL. I wrote in the passenger seat of a rented mini-van on a family road trip with three kids fighting in the back when I was supposed to be navigating and am mira-culously still married. I wrote one-handed while attempting and failing to breastfeed a colicky baby. Once, in desperation with the deadline looming, I even attempted to write holed up in a hotel room while microdosing magic mushrooms which, instead of giving me the creative surge I'd hoped for, just made me fall into a sleep filled with wonderfully vivid dreams but no resulting word count to speak of. That was probably for the best, but still, you know you're chronically exhausted when even psychedelics can't keep you awake after 8 pm.

Like anything a woman does when trying to balance a job and a family and the general perils of modern-day living, this book was eventually completed in random fits and starts, wildly insufficient stolen moments and almost two years after the agreed deadline. To put that into perspective, John Boyle wrote *The Boy in the Striped Pyjamas* in two and a half days. That's embarrassing. But I share my shame because when a woman who has a high-profile career and multiple children does something annoying like publish a book, our natural reaction is to compare ourselves to them. What we perceive, though, is just a half-truth, a highlight reel. We don't see the fails, the imperfection, the often bloody hard work. We don't see all the snapping at their children they did or the fighting with their partner, and we definitely don't see the mess—both literal and figural—they leave behind in the wake of trying to get it done. We just think, 'Bloody hell, she wrote a book this year and I've barely been able to keep the fiddle leaf fig tree alive.' We think, 'How does it come so easy to her?' We think, 'She must really have it all together and also look at her shiny hair why isn't my hair that shiny god I'm so fat.' I'm the worst at this. I once ended up in the wormhole of a parody Marg Simpson Instagram account and found myself unsettled and wanting for days. The last thing I would want this book to do is contribute to the culture of comparison that curses us all. I think it's important for anyone who picks it up to know that the process was a bit of a shitfight and the fact that you're holding it right now—something that is far from perfect, but at least *done*—is somewhat of a miracle.

I know that I've been lucky enough to experience a lot of high-shine, ultra-sparkly, pinch-me moments in my life. As with every woman we might compare ourselves to, it is, of course, mostly surface. This book is an attempt to go behind that glossy façade and show the Hot Mess Express that almost always lies beneath.

PART ONE

eyes

SLIDING DOORS

IT'S THE MID-SEVENTIES. My mum and her best friend, Diane, were attached at the denim-flared hip. They had similar hennaed brown hair and matching gold hoop earrings, just like they'd stepped straight out of an ad for Charlie perfume in *Cleo* magazine. It wasn't much of a surprise to anyone that they fell pregnant with their first babies at the same time—both girls, born just six months apart. So when it came to choosing our own best friend, this spawn of Sydney's answer to Laverne and Shirley didn't have much choice in the matter.

Diane's daughter, Melanie, was everything I wasn't. Blonde to my brunette, street smart to my bookish, supremely confident to my painfully shy. She and I adored each other at all times that we weren't trying to gouge out one another's eyeballs, which was often. Our feelings for each other were intense, as girls' feelings are, and our friendship was wildly complicated, as female friend-ships tend to be. But whether we were leaning more towards love or loathing at any given time, we were completely inseparable and

utterly entwined. We finished each other's sentences. We made our parents buy us matching clothes. We moped dramatically when the constant bickering drove our mothers to try giving us a break from each other. Melanie would go on to feature in all my most significant early memories and play the lead protagonist in every single one of my childhood adventures, so much a part of me that, looking back, I could almost believe that she wasn't really a person in her own right at all but my little-girl equivalent of *Fight Club*'s Tyler Durden, a manifestation of the better, stronger, fiercer, naughtier version of myself I only wished I could be.

Together, we were delightful little sadists. One Good Friday, working hard on a dramatic Mary Magdalene-inspired interpretive dance for our families' feigned enjoyment after Easter brunch, Melanie encouraged me to aggressively force a crown of real garden rose stems onto her stepbrother Sam's head and draw stigmata on his hands and feet in permanent red marker. As with everything, I did what she asked without question. At one point, I wondered if we should remove the thorns from the rose stems first, but I was too scared of Melanie to dare question her—and it did give Sam's Jesus a real air of pained authenticity which I told myself the audience would appreciate. Then we forced the poor kid—also under his stepsister's charismatic spell—to stand with his arms outstretched for hours as though he was hanging on the cross, while we rehearsed, moaning mournfully and flailing around him like Kate Bush in 'Wuthering Heights'.

But most of the time, Melanie was good for me. We were nine when her stepfather got a video camera, a hefty black box

that he had to balance on his shoulder, to capture endless recordings of everyone stopping whatever they were doing to stand still, smile and wave for the camera. One day, breaking out of the Stop, Smile and Wave rut, he seated all the kids in a row and asked us to introduce ourselves, one by one, and tell him what we wanted to be when we grew up. I was desperately timid, so this was my worst imaginable nightmare. I went last and had a few false starts, getting up and sitting down a few times, mortified by the idea of public speaking even when the 'public' was just my own family. It was Melanie who pushed me forward and barked at me encouragingly as I awkwardly half-whispered in the vague direction of the camera that I wanted be the editor of *Dolly*. (It's not a dream I'll ever achieve, only—one day, far in the future—getting as close as deputy editor, which involved enough sorting of the Dolly Doctor letter bag to kill anyone's childhood dreams/innocence.)

Another time, it was Melanie's natural life skill at finding trouble that helped us discover the stack of *Playboys* under her uncle's bed during a game of hide-and-seek at a dinner party in the eighties. With the adults all tipsy on moselle and no TikTok to keep children safely(ish) occupied, this was the sort of thing that happened all the time.

From that moment on, our new favourite game was 'Photographer and Lady', where one of us would sit on the floor busily clicking away with an invisible camera ('Click, click,' we would say, sounding out the word, 'Click, click') while the other sat opposite with her knickers off, bored and impatiently waiting for her turn to do the clicking part. (I don't ever go on to participate

in any actual pornography, but I can only assume this is a fairly true summation of the feelings of the talent involved in the real thing too.)

The two of us spent many hours over many months playing Photographer and Lady, until one night Melanie's mum overheard us in the bath. 'Click, click. Move the bubbles! I can't see anything! Click, click.' She peeked in, curious, and then threw open the door in horror at the sight in front of her. Much of the talk that she and my mum gave us that night is a shameful blur, except for the fact that that it went for so long the bath turned cold. And at the end, a plea that came out as a wail: 'You wouldn't want to end up as lesbians'—Diane dragging out the word 'lez-bee-unz', so we could really take in the full extent of the warning through our shivers—'*would* you?!'

Why she was more appalled by the prospect of raising baby gays instead of trying to work out exactly where this clearly learned behaviour had come from probably says more about the time than anything else. It's 1982, still two years before Culture Club toured Australia and we were all shocked to hear on the 5 pm news that Boy George was homosexual. I was five. I had no idea what a lesbian was, but we'd just learned about vegetarians in school and if it was anything like that, I knew I wanted no part of it. We didn't ever play Photographer and Lady again.

However, unfortunately, we had already introduced many other children to the game over the preceding months and it had become quite the fad in the local area, nicely filling a gap in the time line between our Strawberry Shortcake dolls phase and the launch of the Speak & Spell. Thank god no other parents,

as far as I know, ever found out that a pair of five-year-olds had started a cottage industry of make-believe soft porn among the kids of the eastern suburbs.

Even when she wasn't behind the pretend camera, Melanie ruled me with an iron fist, a little kindergartener Cersei Lannister. Her favourite colour was pink so mine had to be purple, at least as far as I was allowed to state publicly, with only my singlets and knickers reflecting the true me. When she wanted Crystal Barbie for Christmas, I had to resentfully ask Santa for the Day to Night doll. She wore a business suit that, when turned upside down and inside out, became a cocktail dress. It was no iridescent floor-length stole, but it was a feat of engineering—such a pity that it never caught on in sizes for bodies with a BMI that allowed them to actually menstruate. (In years to come, balancing a job and a newborn, I'll often think of it and wish I had my own version, except instead of a fun party frock, the flip side of my polished office look could just be saggy-bummed tracksuit bottoms and a Justin Bieber 'Sorry' tour T-shirt with baby-vom stains on it. What a time saver.)

When we played *Grease,* which was always, Melanie got to be Sandy and I had to be Rizzo. Worse, when we played *Grease 2,* she got to be the supercool Stephanie Zanoni and I had to be Sharon, a Jackie Kennedy-wannabe who gets felt up by her gross boyfriend in a nuclear bunker as he tries to manipulate her into sex by appealing to her sense of patriotism ('It's like we'd be doing it for Disneyland!'). This was a bitter pill to swallow, although one day I'd eventually come to realise that with her ability to withstand that sort of intense sexual pressure, Sharon was quite

the early teen feminist. If I'd only embraced the role with more enthusiasm, I might have learned a few things that would come in handy later on. Sharon, after all, wouldn't even give it up for the Magic Kingdom, whereas sometimes teenage me would pash someone I had no interest in at all, just for a Midori.

Melanie may have been a three-foot-high despot but she was also my most powerful influence, the closest thing I'd ever have to a real-life guru until Covid-19 hit and, like eight million other women in my demographic, I discovered Adriene from *Yoga by Adriene*. My mother was a born nurturer, but she didn't have time to be doling out words of wisdom or sage advice. She was busy surviving—a single mother working multiple jobs at a time just to keep food on the table for me and my brother and sister. She and my father divorced when I was just a baby. I suspect my mum may have just been in it to get herself an exotic child— when I ask her about their relationship, she always gets a sort of befuddled look on her face and says something like, 'Oh, it was the seventies, Indonesians were very fashionable', like she's talking about mood rings or macramé. I have vague recollections of odd weekends spent with my father as a very young child, but they're just flashes of a person, nothing concrete. Once a year or so, he picked me up and took me out to lunch and then on an outing to the Grace Bros toy department, where on the instruction of my mother (who, in her defence, had never received any child support), I would buy the biggest thing I could find—life-sized Care Bears, a ride-on My Little Pony—only to return to the scene of the crime with her later to exchange it for the thing I really wanted, plus a cash bonus.

With my mother preoccupied and bereft of older sisters, it was Melanie I looked to for guidance in life and for wisdom and direction, despite the fact that I was a year ahead of her at school because I was born five days before the end of June enrolment cut-off and she was a December baby.

It was because of those tiny five days that our friendship eventually fell apart. The dynamic between us changed when I started high school and she was still in Year 6. I could no longer blindly accept the authority of a mere primary-school kid who still referred to recess as 'little lunch'. She struggled to maintain dominance over someone who considered herself a woman of the world for not only possessing a New South Wales state transit student card but also knowing how to use it. This shift dramatically affected our established power balance, and our friendship, once so tightly bound, began to slowly unravel. Before I even noticed, Melanie stopped being my other half and had become just another family friend's daughter about whom I heard second-hand stories through my mum, although of course she was never really that.

Then, when we were seventeen, Melanie fell in love with a boy. He was the whole package: ridiculously cute, popular, from a wealthy family, an amazing surfer—and a heroin addict. After a while, besotted in the way only a teenage girl can be, Melanie decided she wanted to try this thing that had such a hold over him, that took him away from her all the time. She loved him and she wanted to be as close to him as it was possible to be, to feel everything that he felt. I wasn't there for any of this, of course, but I heard about it through our mums and I suspect that the

preternatural confidence she was born with made Melanie think there was no way the drug could get a hold on her. She was in charge, as she had always been. She was invincible. I can see why she might have thought that. Even though she wasn't my best friend anymore, I thought she was invincible too.

She was too scared to inject herself, so he did it for her the first time—and he continued to do it for her every time, every day, for the next four years, until he died from an overdose and she had to learn how to do it herself.

Melanie could have been anything, done anything. In the end, her innate power finally showed itself and she managed to beat her addiction. But it took almost twenty years. And a two-decade-long heroin habit tends to get in the way of any other kind of life.

~

Throughout my late teens, Melanie was a constant reminder to me of what might happen if I didn't make the right decision at every step, a cautionary tale playing out like my own *Sliding Doors* alternate reality just a few suburbs away. I didn't always heed the warnings. But underneath all that, she was still my first love and my OG soulmate—the kind whose life is entwined with yours like two acts of the one play, who knows all your secrets and is always by your side, right there with you at your best and brightest and at your worst and most exposed. Losing her friendship was probably the making of me—it wasn't until I didn't live in her illustrious shadow anymore that I worked out who I was, or at least who I wanted to be (and could wear any colour hairband I chose). But even so, without her, I felt somehow untethered,

missing the sort of bind to another person whose mere existence makes you feel safer and more substantial in the world. I didn't realise it as I so easily discarded my connection with her in favour of my fellow Year 7 sophisticates on the train, but I'll spend years searching for a love that could compare to ours again.

SO WHAT ARE YOU, ANYWAY?

MY MOTHER NEVER met a competition she didn't like. It didn't matter to her whether the prize was a new Toyota Celica or a $10 Brashs gift card, she could tell you in twenty-five words or less exactly why she needed it in her life. Little entry envelopes addressed to PO boxes could always be found scattered around our house and her car, flying out of her handbag when she was hunting for a tissue, being shoved into our hands if she suspected we might be going somewhere in the vicinity of a postbox. My siblings and I spent more time helping her to work out radio station mystery sounds than doing our homework and were forced to spend most of our childhoods answering the phone in the morning with the words '2WS is my station'—meaning that anyone calling our house before 9 am had zero to no chance of being answered unless Mum happened to be near the wall phone herself.

I was seven when all her hard graft finally paid off big time with a win of $13,000 in the *Daily Mirror* newspaper's city-wide bingo competition. The result of this unexpected windfall—aside from my first ever awkward picture in the paper, a telling precursor to so many unflattering social pages pictures to come—was that we suddenly become upwardly mobile, moving from the Federation-style semi in Queens Park in Sydney's cosmopolitan, leafy east that we'd rented for almost my entire life, to a newly purchased, dilapidated fibro house on a main road opposite a panelbeater deep in the south-west 'burbs. Winning!

Great Australian Dream aside, the knock-on effect of this for me was that I was forced to move from my small, diverse, inner-city primary school—where my classmates were a mix of Italian, Greek, Chinese, Filipino, Lebanese, Spanish, American and Brazilian (except for the blond, blue-eyed dreamboat David Hall, who I knew I was in a serious long-term relationship with because three times between kindergarten and Year 3 he held my hand on the way to the park for PE) to the *Black Mirror* version in the suburbs, where everyone looked exactly the same and you could be teased mercilessly for having anything as exotic as salami instead of chicken loaf in your sandwich for lunch. This is where I learned that I was different to the other children because a bunch of boys pulled their eyes into slits and told me so about five minutes after I arrived. This was shocking news to me.

~

My father is Indonesian, but because I've never really had much of a relationship with him it genuinely never occurred to me

that I could be anything but a true-blue, ridgy-didge happy little Vegemite. A quick look in the mirror would have told me that I couldn't be more of a mutt. My mum's side of the family, the only one I've ever known, are Irish on one side and Lebanese on the other—aka 'Lebrish'—but culturally they weren't really either. My grandfather's great-grandfather was sent to Australia for the theft of a cow, a crime he was eventually found to be innocent of, but he enjoyed the place so much that he chose not to go home to his wife and children when freed and instead just started himself a new family in the penal colonies. My grandmother's parents moved here from Lebanon before she was born and had refused to ever even discuss the old country, leaving Nanna with nothing to show of her ancestral culture but a large and handsome nose. Both sides had assimilated swiftly and fervently to become as salt-of-the-earth Aussie bogan as they come. They're who I identified as my people: the kind who laughed uproariously at *Hey Hey It's Saturday* together as a family, went to the Chinese buffet at the RSL on special occasions and bought each other scratchies on significant birthdays. (As an adult, I will always hate scratchies, which remind me of all the times as a teenager I desperately hoped for cash in a birthday card and instead ended up with a dirty thumbnail and not a dollar to show for it. I love my family deeply but instant lottery tickets are my version of *Mommy Dearest*'s wire coathangers: 'NO $2 SCRATCHIES, EVER!')

At my old school, everyone had had their differences, so mine were never particularly noticed and definitely never pointed out. After we moved away, the area went on to be well and truly gentrified, but back then the kids there were the children of immigrants,

of single mothers, of families that had three generations living in one home. My Maori stepfather and the fact that sometimes my mum had to work late at her second job so would send our bikie neighbour to pick me up on his Harley barely caused a ripple.

But at this new school, everyone seemed to have just one dad, the same skin colour as them, and a mum who did tuckshop duty twice a week. I stood out, and not because of my gorgeous penmanship or ability to Double Dutch.

Otherness of any kind is the last thing you want as a child. Consequently, from the second I showed up at my new school, I spent every waking moment trying to counter mine. My hair was dead straight, so I convinced my mum to let me get a spiral perm which would takes years to grow out, leaving me with frizzy ends and poker-straight roots for ages after. I surmised at some point that I'd never seen a plump Asian person, so I made it a mission to eat a cream bun every day after lunch. In that white-bread environment, even fat seemed preferable to Asian. Needless to say that neither of these strategies worked in my favour and that I would pay the price for them for years to come.

I might not have thought of myself as Asian, but unfortunately for little self-loathing me, how people identify you is not based on how you feel about yourself on the inside—rather, what you look like plays a pretty significant part. Particularly when you're seven, your personal identity is deeply determined by how other people see you and, in my case, I was never quite sure what they were seeing, exactly. For instance, I vaguely understood from eaves-dropping under tables that the reason my grandfather's crotchety brother Uncle Tom had never liked me was because his eldest son

was killed in Vietnam. I didn't know how that was my fault or why it drove him to leave the room whenever I entered it, but I still managed to feel really bad about it.

~

Eventually I came to accept, if not really embrace, my ethnicity. The lack of a relationship with my father meant I didn't have any connection to the culture, which was a pity, but at least I could appreciate how it gave me hair that didn't need blow-drying and cheeks that made me look younger than my years.

Still, as any bi-racial person will tell you, it's annoying to constantly have to answer the questions 'Where are you from?' and 'What are you, anyway?' It's weird to be made to stand around awkwardly while someone treats your ethnic background like a fun guessing game, throwing out country after country like they can't decide what they want to order from Menulog for dinner ('Korean! Wait . . . Japanese! No. Chinese!'). In my case as well, looking racially ambiguous always seems to be an open door to personal questions I can't always give a neat answer to. It might start out as innocently as 'What's your nationality?', but it soon leads to 'Do you speak Bahasa?', and before I know it, I'm explaining my entire dysfunctional family history to the nice Uber driver.

~

I haven't experienced much blatant racism in my life, but I have experienced a lot of the more covert kind—those unintentional, unwitting comments that grate in the moment but that you just

learn to live with. For example, I'm constantly being told that I look like Lucy Liu. She's gorgeous and that would be great if I looked like her *in any way at all* but I don't, making it just a more complimentary take on the 'all Asians look alike to me' trope. Also, people generally—incorrectly—assume my mother must be the Asian half of my parentage, which is classic sexual racism because god forbid that a white woman would want to procreate with an Asian man, although of course it would be perfectly understandable the other way around because Asian women are hypersexualised whether it suits them or not. Early on in my dating life, I got into the habit of sniffing around any boy who was ever interested in me, on the lookout for potential Asian fetishism. If I ever learned that a guy I was seeing had dated another Asian-blooded girl before me or had once kissed one, or if he was a bit too into anime or had ever taken a mildly suspect boys' trip to Thailand, it was an immediate deal-breaker and I bolted, positive that within days he'd be trying to eat sashimi off my naked body.

When friends jokingly refer to me as being 'Asian-inspired', or 'fusion' (the unspoken allusion being that being part-white is somehow superior to being purely Asian) or once as 'Asian-ish with boobs', I'm not insulted exactly, but it is dehumanising. (And, actually, I am insulted by the boob one, but as a woman rather than an Asian.)

The Lucy Liu comments and others like them might appear to be benign, but over time they add up in your head. They leave you with a heightened awareness of race and perception, even if you're not experiencing prejudice in its more obvious forms.

They have an effect. The result is an aversion to stereotypes that somehow *still* prevents me from carrying a top-handled bag, even when it's Gucci. And no matter how innocuously the comment is delivered, or by whom, I'm not hearing it for what it is anyway. I'm just hearing those boys back on that first day at my new school, pulling their eyes into slits.

~

I was in my mid-twenties and mostly over my identity struggles when my mum called with some news. Being the world's most considerate human, she'd kept in semi-regular contact with my father over the years in case there ever came a time when I might want to get to know him. (People who've grown up loving both parents equally never understand the genuine indifference of a child to a parent they've never known, but the only time I ever felt anything like a paternal yearning was when Kelly's dad showed up to graduation on *Beverly Hills 90210*. That really got me in the feels. But my own dad showing up to dinner once a decade? Not so much.)

She informed me breathlessly that my cousin was getting married and that we'd both been invited to the wedding. Apparently my father had never really been all that forthcoming with his family about the extent of his estrangement from his wife and daughter, and twenty-three years since we last lived under the same roof, he'd called her up out of the blue requesting that we fly to Jakarta with him to play happy families and put on a show. Mum, ever the prize enthusiast, was giddy with the news that we'd won an all-expenses-paid trip to Indonesia.

I was nervous about meeting my other family and had no idea what to expect, so it was a surprise when we landed and were met at the airport by our allocated bodyguard. It turned out that my cousin was marrying Indonesian President Megawati Sukarnoputri's son. The wedding itself was a state occasion, attended by 6000 people over three days. Because we were family, my mother and I were taken to a boutique which was heaving with women of all ages, bustling around laughing and yelling chaotically, and fitted in complicated national dress. There were multiple outfits to wear in different moments, all of which required an assistant to help us go to the bathroom. ('Best not to drink too much water,' my fitter advised helpfully later on that night as she reattached me to my skirt for the third time in an hour, leaving me to panic about dehydration in the 42-degree heat.) Traditional wigs were attached and Dior 5 Couleurs eye make-up was applied with some flair by a woman who had clearly not moved on since the heady days of Studio 54. My Lebrish mother looked like the most offensive exhibit of touristic cultural appropriation you'd ever seen. But I looked in the mirror, high on the love of the brand-new, completely different, but deeply kind and welcoming family that I was suddenly surrounded by, and I saw what everyone else had been seeing my whole life. And for the first time, I wasn't uncomfortable with it at all.

YOUTH-DEW

THE STORY OF Youth-Dew is legendary in beauty circles. Before it came along, perfume was something that was only given as a gift, and often chosen by men. I generally won't let anyone else choose a dressing for my side salad, so this seems unimaginable to me. It was apparently also offensive to the great Estée Lauder, early feminist, who wanted to create a perfume that women bought for themselves. But this wild and dangerous idea, apparently, was a harder sell than she'd imagined. So one day, being the early guerrilla marketing genius that she was, she went into a New York department store and 'dropped' a bottle on the floor, drawing women from across the store to ask what the scent was and where they could buy it. It was the first ever viral beauty sensation, the Kylie Jenner Lip Kits for the 1950s woman.

I might have only been a child but I already knew the perfume as my nanna's 'signature scent'. If there had been such a thing as social media at the time, my nanna would have followed, liked, subscribed and been on the waitlist for Youth-Dew. She was a

big fan. The fragrance was originally marketed as a bath oil and that's how nanna still used it, drenching herself in the stuff from top to toe. Because it was her smell, it made me feel safe and loved, but sometimes it was a bit difficult to breathe in her presence, so redolent was she of oriental spice. The advantage of this is that it meant we knew she was coming seconds before she actually appeared, which was not a bad thing. She didn't ever get angry at us, her beloved grandchildren, but it was always good to know when a dictatorial matriarch like her was coming, lest she wrangle you into watching your second cousin's home video from her family trip to Bali three years ago. Again.

As the child of a single mother, I spent a lot of time with my grandmother. She was the primary influence in my life, in every sense other than fashion. Nanna was not known for her style or good taste, although she was actually big into make-up, especially rouge (which was what she called blush), pronounced in her strong Australian drawl with a hard G so that the word sounded nothing like its French origins. I'd be happily pottering around the house, accompanying one of my Barbies on a disappointing blind date with my little brother's He-Man, and like a perfumed velociraptor she'd appear out of the blue—with a speed surprising for someone of her girth—to attack me unawares and smear my cheeks with the pot of lurid reddish pink cream she kept topped up from Jan, the Avon lady who lived three doors down. I can't tell you when it started, but there are photos of me in her arms as a newborn with a suspiciously flushed complexion, so it's possible she was zhooshing me up right from birth. It wasn't until I was about eleven and could more easily escape her prodding fingers

that she stopped, although I'd continue to catch her giving disappointed looks to my bare cheeks for years to come.

Nanna had a tendency to bad taste, to a trampy style that didn't suit either her strong moral compass or her body shape, but that she would have desperately loved to channel through me. She was the only grandmother I knew who was constantly telling her granddaughter to put on more make-up and wear shorter skirts. It also irritated her to high heaven how much I enjoyed a book. She thought it was unhealthy. In this and other things, I was a constant concern. It drove her crazy, all that wretched reading and disappearing to the bloody library in the school holidays when I could have been home watching *Donahue* on the sofa with her.

What I wanted, though, was just to be living a much more exciting life than I was. While Nanna was chasing me around the house with the rouge pot trying to put just a little bit of colour into my cheeks, in my head I was always somewhere else—running through the streets of The Rocks listening to children playing a terrifying game called Beatie Bow, learning about love and loss in the magical world of Terabithia, discovering the lands temporarily parked atop the oldest and tallest tree in the Enchanted Wood and (in my less worthy moments) as a high school student in a town called Sweet Valley, deciding which Wakefield sister I wanted to be friends with most (Jessica, of course). I walk-read, bumping into people, pets and walls as I went. I'd read a book in a single sitting, finishing it under the doona by torchlight, then immediately starting again from the beginning. I spent a couple of glorious months as an eight-year-old reading *The Chronicles of Narnia* in the order they were written, and then again in the

order they were intended to be read, only occasionally coming up for air, Space Food Sticks or *Young Talent Time*.

All this worried my nanna endlessly (most things worried Nanna endlessly, in particular: airplane travel, dogs let off leashes, open curtains after dusk), but she loved me regardless. Sometimes I could even get her to join me in a book. One summer holidays in my late teens, we read *The Bronze Horseman* at the same time, sitting out on her balcony. There's no-one who has ever been more riveted by the written word than Nanna was throughout its famously never-ending sex scene, her avid page-turning punctuated with audible little noises that went from surprised to titillated to scoffing and back as the reunion sex between the two protagonists went on and on and on and on. Afterwards, we needed to share a little glass of port.

Despite all the reading, which she was positive would somehow be the death of me, I was the first grandchild and also Nanna's favourite. When it came to the rest of our family, those sweet little dumdums, the two of us ran the show. Together we gossiped and conspired, scheming to get our way, choosing where and how we wanted to celebrate holidays and other people's birthdays, what we wanted to eat and do and who we wanted there. We put as much effort into our domestic plots as any of the characters on *Days of Our Lives*, her favourite show, which I'm pretty sure she genuinely believed was the first ever reality show centred on real-life people from the actual town of Salem. But when it came to familial manipulation, Victor Kiriakis had nothing on us.

This brazen alliance with the most important member of our family gave me a misguided sense of my own power. Sometimes

it went to my head, especially at Christmas. While Nanna was in charge of the food, I decided on the table settings, announced when it was time to pull the crackers and—after the year one of my aunts ruined it for everyone by playing her John Williamson *Christmas in Australia* CD on repeat—dictated the music, which was almost always Bing Crosby, except after my pa died because then it just made Nanna cry. Most importantly, I was in charge of which of the presents from under the tree was given to a receiver to unwrap before allowing anyone to move on to the next. It was a self-appointed role, but one everyone accepted without debate. I took it very seriously. As our family grew, with more and more noisy cousins, eventually I got a small festive megaphone to help me do the job. I thought it added a certain gravitas to the proceedings. Not everyone in the family enjoyed this element as much as I did, but it's not my fault if some people are intimidated by a powerful woman.

The only thing Nanna and I disagreed on when it came to Christmas was presentation. My nanna was a little roly-poly ball of pure love, generous with hugs and kind words and golden syrup dumplings. But aesthetics were not her thing. She left all that rubbish to her older sisters. The eldest, Mary, was a hairdresser in her day, and if not necessarily elegant (most of my memories of when she would come to stay with us involve her standing in front of the gas heater lifting her skirt up to let the hot air circulate around her bottom, which was ample), she was at least polished in a Queen Mum kind of a way. The middle sister, Sadie, was a vixen, a glamorous old bird who had—as whispered to me in secret by my pa after too many rums one Anzac Day dawn service—been

'a bit cuddly' in her youth. She'd lost all the excess weight and then some to win the heart of a handsome soldier named Pat and she kept it off her whole life to keep her man. I don't know how that worked out for her, because by the time I knew him Uncle Pat was well established as a monosyllabic couch potato who sat in a permanent cloud of rollie smoke, but Auntie Sadie must have thought he was worth it because she always looked the part. She had long Rita Hayworth-esque waves, home-dyed a vivid, brassy red of the kind not found in nature. She seemed ancient to me her entire life (not that you could ever dare speak to her of her age) but every morning she got up, put a sheer white negligee over her matching sheer white nightie, slipped on her everyday shoes—a pair of three-inch white stiletto pumps—and did fifty step-ups on the front porch. After her work-out, she put on her uniform of spray-on skinny jeans, one of a wide variety of clingy sweaters, garish red lipstick and, as she got older, gigantic, bug-like black sunglasses. She continued this routine well into her nineties. At her funeral, a family friend told me a story about visiting in the middle of a chilly Goulburn winter to find Sadie hanging washing on the line. The friend, having never seen Sadie out of heels, was shocked to see her wearing ugg boots. She helped her hang out the rest of her washing and followed her inside for a cup of tea. It wasn't until they were sitting down in the living room that Sadie removed the ugg boots only to reveal that she'd been wearing her stilettos *inside them* the whole time. If that's not commitment to style, I don't know what is.

My nanna had no time for such shenanigans. She enjoyed a sensible slipper shoe and a haircut that made her look like a

caricature of a nineties lesbian. When it came to Christmas, her priority was to feed, not to make things look pretty. She grunted with impatient irritation when I took her away from whisking the gravy to help me find the good cutlery. She unthinkingly ruined the table I spent hours styling with a last-minute plonking down of a beige Tupperware microwave dish right in the middle, just in time for the photos. But I was forced to bite my tongue, because no matter how imperious I felt towards the rest of the family, Nanna was the real Queen and I was just her lackey with some status by association.

In years to come, when I became a beauty editor, one of the best perks—alongside enough pots of Crème de la Mer to use on my flaky knees and bottles of Chanel Coco Mademoiselle to use as a room spray—was to be able to supply Nanna with an unending supply of Youth-Dew, cream blush and fancy skin cream, unimaginable luxuries for someone who left school after Year 5 and could feed a table of twelve on a single roast chook. She went overnight from someone who was happy to slap hand cream on her face to someone who had more $300 tubs of moisturiser on her dressing table than Elizabeth Taylor, although I could never tell her what they cost or they would have all degraded while she saved them for good.

~

I was thirty-five when my nanna died, older than many people are when they lose their grandparents, but it still felt like our time together wasn't nearly enough. Nothing is ever the same. With her death, I lost my home base, my confidante, my moral

compass, my 6 pm phone gossip buddy. I no longer had a North Star. She passed away in August, so within a few months it fell to me to step up and take on Christmas alone, and I channelled my grief into the day. Wrapping paper was coordinated with a strict colour theme that I briefed the family on beforehand and which no-one paid any attention to, forcing me to whisk away pressies as they were hauled inside from car boots in black garbage bags and laundry baskets and rewrap them to my liking. Table settings were perfected. The food, rather than being heaving legs of crackling pork just pulled from the oven and tray after tray of roast potatoes, became a more seasonally appropriate mix of cold meats and pretty, fresh salads, and while it was still delicious, I couldn't help but feel that it had lost some of its soul. I tried to fill a Nanna-shaped hole in our lives with as much Pinterest perfection as I could muster, but without those random bits of Tupperware ruining all the photos, it could never be as good.

It's a two-hour drive from my office to the hospital where Nanna lay dying, and despite breaking every possible traffic rule, I got there too late and missed being able to say goodbye to her by about half an hour. I kissed her still-warm cheek and put a fresh bottle of Youth-Dew in her hand. She was being cremated so I don't know what happened to it, but I like to imagine her up in heaven, doused heavily in her signature scent, chasing the gods around, just trying to put some colour in their cheeks.

GENERATION GAP

MY FIRST PRIMARY school was essentially an entire Catholic universe all squeezed onto a single inner-city block. There was the school, which was tiny, despite having gone from infants-only to a full primary a few years prior. There was a church. And there was a presbytery, called Father's House, which was bigger than both the school and church buildings and placed right smack bang in the middle of the school grounds, a questionable choice of real estate positioning to say the least. There was an actual convent over the back fence, called the Little Sisters of the Poor, and the nuns—with their mysterious ways and sweet dispositions—briefly made me want to be one, until I realised that my disposition was in no way as sweet and, decisively, my full-faced bone structure completely ill-suited to a habit. (My mother, who was caned by less kindly sisters for being left-handed every single day of her schooling career yet suffered from enough Stockholm syndrome she sent her firstborn straight back to Catholic school, was much relieved.) Squished like afterthoughts among this Greatest Hits

of Catholicism were a couple of courtyards, one at the front of the school and one at the back. They were pitched to prospective parents as playgrounds, except you couldn't do much playing in them because they were made of the roughest kind of asphalt— the violently skin-destroying kind with loose black bits that are impossible to remove from bloodied hands and knees. The only sign of life in this woefully inadequate concrete jungle was a giant fig tree whose roots were breaking through the asphalt, taking up much-needed ground space and leaving its sticky fruit all over our shoes and often our bottoms if we dared attempt to sit on the ground anywhere in its vicinity.

Looming over it all, taking up almost the entire length of the back 'playground', which also moonlighted as the carpark, was a perfect hill made up of the lushest green grass you could ever imagine, the Prada of turf. This mossy lawn to the side of the presbytery was Father's Grass, larger than both of our asphalt deathtraps combined, which we children were permitted to look at but must never, ever step upon. It wasn't cut off by a fence or barrier of any kind, nothing to actually stop us from stepping on it, but no child that I know would have ever dared nonetheless. We were all reverent about Father's Grass—even the naughtiest boys among us, the ones who talked during mass so would obviously grow up to be drug dealers and degenerates. We didn't know much in Year 1, but we knew without a doubt that anyone who puts their grubby little feet upon the lawn was certain to be struck down by a God whose greatest pet peeve was children touching His Grass. One day during recess, I mindlessly removed a blade while sitting on the low brick retaining wall at

its base. I immediately dropped to my knees in front of everyone and said ten Hail Marys without being asked, just in case. And I wondered why I wasn't popular.

One Easter, the unthinkable happened. Father O'Donoghue, a mostly terrifying human, allowed the teachers to organise an Easter egg hunt on the Holy Knoll. Unsure of what to do with such liberty, we started out carefully, daintily tiptoeing around so as to not mar the lush turf with our unhallowed presence, politely moving ferns and peeking behind carefully trimmed oleanders to gather the chocolate goodness. But eventually, inevitably, our base childish natures overcame us. That's when the running began, then the tripping, then the falling, and the rolling. I found myself at the bottom of a pile of kids with Jenny Campbell's foot in my face and some dislodged turf in my mouth and before any of us knew what was happening, the egg hunt was called to a premature halt and back up went the invisible barrier between us and Father's Grass, never to be breached again.

~

We were not very diligent Catholics in my family—we only went to mass at Christmas and Easter, we gave up things for Lent that we didn't really care about in the first place, we always forgot that it was Good Friday until after we'd finished eating bacon with our breakfast—but it still played a big part in my cultural identity. For one, it informed my primary personality attribute—self-reproach—and gave me something to rebel against once I was old enough to make up my own mind. Even so, I still can't bring myself to throw out any of the holy cards I ever received for

being the first one in my class to learn the more obscure prayers in primary school. I have a lot of them, mostly because if you nailed, say, Hail Holy Queen before anyone else, you also got your choice of a chocolate bar, which I personally found incredibly motivating. I can still recite the Act of Contrition by rote at a moment's notice if you dangle a Flake in front of me.

When I grew up and had children of my own, I didn't baptise any of them but I did send the older ones to a Christian high school, less for its spiritual ethos than because we got sucked in by the stadium seating in the hall and a couple of suspiciously well-spoken and polite Year 12s. We're easily impressed. Not so much the kids, who both turned out to be decidedly atheist. One was so bothered by the constant chapel and Christian Studies classes that he waged a campaign to allow him to transfer to the local public school, eventually getting his way in Year 8 with a Google Slides deck presenting the argument 'Science is my Jesus'. For now, I'm just thankful that the third has yet to turn to Satanism or start a cult of his own, but I guess there's still time.

The lack of any kind of organised religion in their lives is my decision, but I still find it weird that the lapsed but niggling cultural Catholicism of my childhood isn't part of their identities, that they don't have all the same childhood points of reference as me—like making my first communion in my creepy little bride's dress, the torture of not being able to open Christmas presents or eat Easter eggs until after mass, the terror of confession, having conversations with God and making him promises I was never going to be able to keep in exchange for minor blessings like a netball win. It is, I imagine, a little bit like when you raise your

child in another country and they grow up with a different accent to you or don't know what Paddle Pops are. It also makes me mildly worried for their futures. If you don't know the God who bores you silly at church, what's to stop you thinking he's a fun new idea and joining a religious sex cult later on in your formative searching years?

But that's just one of the many things I don't have in common with my children. They've all got penises, for example—*every goddamn one of them*. And while there's a part of raising boys that I think I've got down pretty well—that is, the conscious putting of good, emotionally evolved men into the world—there's another side that doesn't come so naturally to me. I loathe playing with dinosaurs and trains. I don't do wrestling. I live in absolute dread of the park, unless there's rosé and a chicken and almond finger-sandwich involved. I'm only good at Lego the first time you build a new set, when there are instructions to follow or, better yet, when the kids get bored and go to bed so I can finish it all alone and methodically without anyone to get in my way. I can't freestyle build from my imagination. Actually, there was a day I made a mid-sized Lego minion and they all still talk about that one time I was good at Lego years later. I can't tell them I secretly locked myself in the bathroom and watched a YouTube tutorial, the lie has gone too far. On the other hand, you will never see me look sadder than passing by a wall of Sylvanian Families in a toyshop. Those tiny lolly stands! Those tiny boats! All those tiny hedgehogs in their tiny snazzy outfits! It's exactly the same face I pull in Valentino. I want it all so badly but the circumstances of my actual life just won't allow it to be so.

We're different in other ways too. Like many modern parents in the age of the Goop podcast, I feed my children a diet made up of its fair share of wholegrain and superfoods, and a notable lack of the Coola-flavoured cordial that must still make my blood run a deep, dark, flavour-of-unknown-origin green. I ate so many white bread, mystery meat and tomato sauce sandwiches as a child that I'm pretty sure those fleshy parts where my triceps should be are primarily made up of pure unsliced devon, the kind that comes whole and wrapped in plastic with little metal ties on each end. No amount of Tracy Anderson can do anything about the mucilaginous sandwich meat that makes up my guns.

There's also the complicated matter of privilege. I grew up without much of anything—except love, which of course is enough, but not in the opinion of a teenage girl who spent her time almost exclusively immersed in glossy magazines full of *stuff*. Not that we ever went hungry or were completely bereft of treats and nice things. Sometimes my uncle would win big at the TAB and show up, stumbling and forgetting our names, with takeaway Chinese. Honey king prawns meant a trifecta had been on the cards. He wasn't the best gambler, so they were special occasions. Another time, *Daily Mirror* bingo not being her only success story, my mum won a trip to Disneyland from a Channel 9 competition. The prize was for flights, accommodation and park tickets, so our family and friends all chipped in to help her out with food and spending money. She did a really good job of hiding from us how hard it must have been for her to make ends meet, let alone keep me in a wide variety of ink-hued tencel jeans, but that didn't change the fact that we lived in a

house and a street I was so embarrassed of that I'd get friends to drop me off ten minutes up the road.

My children are not at the getting-a-BMW-for-your-seventeenth-birthday level, but in comparison to my own childhood, they may as well be. Takeaway doesn't represent a trifecta to them so much as it does a Tuesday and that their parents didn't get home from work in time to get to a supermarket, often for the second time in a week. They have their own frequent flyer cards. We live in a nice house, not palatial but definitely not one that would necessitate giving your mates a fake address. Still, Scout often complains that we don't live in a mansion. Though this is the same kid who, when asked by his teacher why he was taking so long to write the word 'car', told her he was trying to work out how to spell 'Lamborghini', so he's clearly on his own path.

I find all that hard to sit with. So much of my motivation stemmed from a place of hunger for something more. No-one wants to raise entitled arseholes. I don't even want to raise complacent arseholes. My children are male, white(ish) and live in a part of the world considered one of the most beautiful places on earth. Are they motivated to have goals, drive and ambition, or will they just spend their young adulthoods sitting around watching YouTube and waiting for me to die so they can hock off all my Saint Laurent handbags?

I want them to have to work for things, I want them to have to strive and I definitely don't want them to be spoiled. At the same time, I've already lived my own deprived childhood and now I would like to enjoy for myself all the possible perks on offer to me in this life. This can lead to conflicting emotions

and inconveniences. If we're flying somewhere and are lucky enough to be enjoying an airline lounge, I'll proceed to order all the champagne and ice-cream sundaes, but I don't want them to think that this is normal so I simultaneously ruin the fun of the experience for us and everyone around us by harping on at them that the day will come soon enough when they're travelling alone and jostling outside for McNuggets like I did until I'd worked hard and long and was fortunate enough to have earned this, *if* they're even able to afford to travel at all which they definitely won't be if they don't improve that History grade from a C to an A. It's a downer of a way to kick off a family holiday, but if they can't have deprivation as their motivation, I'll make sure they at least have fear.

Some of these differences can possibly be put down to the times, rather than any sort of economic advantage. Families didn't travel in the eighties except to visit grandparents in England or maybe to Bali or Fiji, coming home with jangly braided hair and a rainbow collection of beaded T-shirts. They definitely didn't travel the way we do now (pre-Covid), where half of Sydney seems to pop off to Puglia for the European summer. And back then, everyone ate like bogans, across the board. Eighties Australia was just not a sophisticated or stylish place, regardless of socio-economic status. We *all* enjoyed a Coon and cabanossi toothpick at a backyard soiree. *All* the dads looked a little like paedophiles.

My children are so much more life-savvy than I was at the same age. I was shy and in a permanent state of embarrassment unless I was around people I knew well and sometimes even then. They're clever conversationalists and good at witty repartee with

anyone they happen to meet. From the youngest ages, they've been comfortable and confident enough to explain their symptoms to the doctor, to ask the waitress themselves for a kombucha on the rocks and to inform me sagely of my responsibilities as a parent and their rights as children when they feel I'm getting it wrong. While I accepted anything an adult told me blindly, they question everything, annoyingly aware of their opinions and moral stances, and this started seemingly from the moment they could talk. They definitely wouldn't have hesitated to walk all over Father's Grass, to wriggle their toes into the soft, lush carpet of green and sink their heels into the soil. I really wish I had too.

EDITOR'S LETTERS

MUM PULLED UP outside the local St Vincent de Paul. I sighed dramatically. Vinnie's was her happy place. She'd been a vintage expert since it was just called second-hand and she still lives for a trawl, coming home with all sorts of treasures and finds that she shows off, proudly announcing the original retail values as she goes. I spent a lot of time as a teen choosing to sit outside in the car reading a book or perfecting my open-palm fringe tease in the rear-vision mirror rather than sniffing around another op shop with her. She never let it show but I know it must have been a disappointment to not to be able to share this passion of hers with me. She probably had dreams of a daughter with whom she could paw through musty boxes of old stuff, lifting our heads only to yell 'Eureka!' upon the discovery of a mint-condition seventies glomesh clutch. Instead, she got stuck with some brat who just longed for a brand-new striped Sportsgirl tote.

I will never get good at vintage shopping. I don't have the eye for it. The smell of mothballs gives me a headache. I can't

rummage: the lack of order and the fear that I might miss some special morsel of fashion gold among the chaos gives me anxiety. None of my stylish adult friends have this affliction but rather than being annoyed by their skills, as I was with my mum, I envy it. My friend Sheree, in particular, can be driving through a dead-beat town in the middle of nowhere and somehow manage to find the only genuine 1950s Chanel skirt in the Southern Hemisphere on sale for $20. I can be in Paris in front of a curated selection of clothes hung by colour with five-centimetre gaps between each hanger and still get overwhelmed and need to take a mental break over a Nutella crepe. Drop me in a market anywhere other than at the clear beginning or end and I'll break out in a sweat; I need an ordered traverse that guarantees I will cover all ground because I need to be very thorough when I shop. Sometimes I don't even have the energy to go online because I know that if I start looking at dresses on Net-a-Porter, I won't be able to stop until I have looked at all ninety-three pages of them, not including sale. Truly, it's debilitating.

There was one thing that I did love about my mum's missions: the piles of magazines she brought home for me, back issues of *Dolly* and *Cleo* that I pored over for hours and kept in enormous piles next to my bed that got taller and more treacherous every week, leading me ever closer to being tragically killed in the night by a glossy paper avalanche. I didn't care that they'd been read a thousand times by the time I got hold of them or that they were sometimes years out of date. To me, they were reference books, timeless tomes to be treasured and studied, *Encyclopaedia Britannica*s of the grown-up world I longed to be a part of.

I loved the smell of the paper, the stories being told via the photo shoots, the mysterious masthead pages with jobs that will never be explained to me by any school careers advisor. What did a 'picture editor' do? What sort of amazing sign did one have to be born under to be called the 'beauty director'?

I knew all the different mastheads individually and thought of them as my friends, each with its own personality and qualities that it brought to our relationship. *Dolly* was the partner-in-crime, the best friend I hadn't had since Melanie and I drifted apart; *Cleo* was the fun-loving older sister I wished I had; and *Cosmo* gave me intoxicating glimpses of the grown-up woman—with a career and an actual sex life—I might be one day. Their voices spoke to me as clearly as if they were real, live people rather than perfectly bound stacks of 80-gsm paper that were so out of date that even Chrissy's Cutz at Miranda Fair had no use for them anymore. But I couldn't get enough, and while buying them new was a luxury my mother could never afford, she was happy to bring me home a stack for 20 cents each week from the Rockdale Trash & Treasure.

While my friends would turn straight to 'Dolly Doctor' and its unrequited crush-focused neighbour 'What Should I Do?', it was the editor's letters that I spent all of my time obsessing over. They made this fantasy world feel real—they helped me realise that magazines were made by actual people. *Dolly*, as I perceived it from its editor's letters, was a world of celebrity interviews, breakfast cereal obsessions and a magical thing called the beauty cupboard, full of free(!!) Lip Smackers. The women who worked there seemed nothing like the adults that I knew, who went to

work behind a bar at the RSL or in shops selling Bali dresses alongside Orgasmatron head scratchers in the local shopping centre and watched the minute hand until clock-off time. The editor's letters told me nothing of deadlines or management politics, long hours at their desks or office misogyny. As far as I could gather, these guys were having a Monday to Friday slumber party and I knew very early on into my magazine obsession that just reading them would never be enough. I wanted in.

Magazines conveniently combined the only two hobbies I ever had: Barbies and books. At eleven, I still spent hours styling my Barbies, making up complicated backstories and big, important lives for them. I gave them all the drama I could only long for, stuck there in my bedroom, sitting on the floor with my back against the door so my little brother and sister couldn't come in and interrupt. Playing with the dolls was something I only ever did alone and in absolute secret, and I held on to them for much longer than was considered socially acceptable. I pretty much went straight from Skipper to sex in one terrifying developmental leap.

In much the same way, I played out all my escapist fantasies through books, letting them transport me from what I perceived to be the drudgery of the life that I'd been born to into other worlds that were much more suited to my temperament. When Amy March despaired, 'I hate poverty, and don't mean to bear it a minute longer than I can help', I knew exactly how she felt, except that it wasn't more money that I cared about so much as it was *specialness*. I just wanted a grander life than the one I had. But instead of needing to marry a rich man to fix my situation, like poor lime-less Amy, I was just hoping to find out that

I was actually the long-lost daughter of Olivia Newton-John. My nanna, that beloved, straight-shooting matriarch who had barely left her house since 1983 but knew the ways of the world, said I had airs about me. As usual, she was right.

PART TWO

brain

PART TWO

brain

PLANET FASHION

IN THE GLORY days of publishing and prior to a hot wardrobe and an Instagram account being considered a legitimate career path, every girl who had an even passing interest in fashion wanted to work in magazines. As a result, they tended to be staffed with girls from wealthy, connected, Eastern Suburbs families, partly because their dads ran in the right circles to help them get an edge in, and partly because they were the only ones could afford to live on magazine wages and still dress in top to toe Morrissey Edmiston. It was a career path for the privileged and the pretty. I definitely wasn't the first and I wasn't sure yet if I was the second. This meant that my one and only opportunity to break into mags would be through work experience in Year 10, and I was itching for it. Every time I read about *Dolly* work experience girls in the magazine, I felt sick with envy. They got to meet visiting celebrities, like John Stamos, and try all the new kinds of ice creams that got sent into the office. It was almost like they were part of the real team. And then there were all

those Lip Smackers. It sounded to me like a week-long, school-endorsed trip to teenage Disneyland.

I knew doing work experience at *Dolly* was as popular as being inside a Goss brothers sandwich and that you needed to book well in advance. I started nagging the school careers advisor at the beginning of Year 7, but she couldn't give me the dates until Year 9—by which time I was genuinely worried that the only place I'd be able to get into would be the local Darrell Lea factory (actually considered quite the glamorous work experience get in my local area). I was so fixated on work experience that I would go on to remember those dates—May 23 to 27—my entire life, which says something from the woman who, as an adult, still has to silently recite a little rhyme each time she's called upon to remember her second son's date of birth.

As soon as I got home that afternoon, I unwound the beige rotary extension cord attached to our home phone and disappeared with them both into my bedroom to call Australian Consolidated Press, the company that owned *Dolly*. I couldn't have been more ready to lock down my future.

An older woman answered the phone. This confused me a little as I had gotten the number directly from the magazine and assumed the phone would be answered by one of the *Dolly* team themselves, each of whom I knew intimately from my years of studying both the editor's letters and those funny little notes in parentheses from the 'Ed' that ran in the middle of the features. (For a very long time, I assumed there must have been a boy named Ed on the team, whose role it was just to comment pithily on the articles. *Now that's a job*, I thought.) At the very least,

I thought it might get picked up by a visiting cast member from *Home & Away*, just passing through.

The receptionist transferred the call. My heart pounded. And then the phone was answered by a girl whose name I recognised as the editorial assistant. I knew from my studies that she was obsessed with Coco Pops and had a West Highland White Terrier called Mattie and I could not have been more excited if NKOTB's Joey McIntyre had been on the end of the line himself.

I composed myself and asked about the dates in question. She answered as if by rote, as if unaware that she was about to break my heart into a million little pieces: 'I'm sorry, we're all booked out for next year, would you like to try *Cleo*?'

I was devastated and deeply bitter, convinced that this would never have happened if my mum had been able to send me to private school where they wore cute straw boaters and would definitely be well-planned enough for their students to be able to get into their work experience of choice.

I was put through to *Cleo*. The editorial assistant there, who I didn't know as intimately because *Cleo* had never been in my life plan, seemed very nice and put me on hold while she consulted a book. 'I'm sorry, we're all booked that week. Would you like to try *Elle*?'

Crushed, I could just about grunt my reply. I'd barely heard of *Elle*—as far as I was concerned, Country Road was the epitome of aspirational fashion—and, besides, by this point I'd pretty much given up on life.

The phone rang again. The editorial assistant at *Elle* was a lot less chipper and her tone quite a bit more intimidating, but the

week was free and she booked me in. I was just happy to have somewhere to go that wouldn't leave me smelling like liquorice at the end of the day. And it was in the same building as *Dolly*. That night, I consoled myself by imagining that the *Dolly* editor, Marina Go, would see me in the lift and just know I was meant to join her team. 'You'll need to leave your pathetic public school immediately,' she'd insist, and after serious consideration, of course I would. (Disappointingly, the fantasy didn't come true, but Marina would end up being my boss one day . . . 24 years later.)

The year took forever. I went to a selective school and upon starting there had quickly realised that being the smartest in your primary school meant nothing once you were in a grade with other people who were all also the smartest in their primary schools. In Year 7, I'd suddenly found myself at the bottom of the class after years of being at the top, and as someone who didn't like to do anything unless I knew I was going to be good at it—hence why you'll never catch me at F45—this succeeded in making me give up on school completely. To me, my secondary education was just a transitional phase I was being forced to endure between birth and my almost definite illustrious magazine career.

For my first day on the job, I wore my usual weekend uniform of a favourite purple miniskirt that had been my mother's in the sixties and a pair of scuffed Doc Marten school shoes that I wore everywhere with everything. It didn't cross my mind to dress differently to go to work at an international fashion magazine than I would to hang out at a shopping centre food court. I was completely unaware of designers or trends, beyond the schoolgirl kind—such as at what height it was currently considered cool to

wear one's socks—which existed purely in their own microcosm as unrelated to the runway as it was possible to be.

I was shepherded into the office by the editorial assistant, who appeared just as uninterested as she sounded on the phone, past the seemingly terrifying, classically cool editor, Debbie Coffey, and handed unceremoniously to a fashion assistant. The fashion assistant immediately shoved some Chanel shopping bags into my hands, gave me a cab charge and the address of a studio a few blocks away and instructed me to deliver the bags directly to the fashion director there and stay as long as she needed me. She pointed at the bags before I left and hissed, 'Guard them with your life.' There wasn't a hint of jest in her tone. I was suitably petrified.

Out on Park Street, I managed to somehow hail a cab. It was maybe the third taxi I'd ever been in in my life, the first without my mum. I was running on pure adrenaline, convinced I'd be mugged if I stood on the street a minute longer than necessary. I didn't have any idea what was in the bags or what it was worth—I wouldn't have believed it if I did—but I knew that if I lost one of them, I'd be having to take extra shifts in the lotto shop I worked at on weekends for the rest of my life and my odds of a future magazine career would go from already slim to definitely none.

After what felt like hours but according to my Swatch watch was about four and a half minutes, I arrived at the studio in Surry Hills giddy with butterflies. Later, I'd go on to shoot at that same studio for many years and every single time I'd walk in, I'd be taken right back to that first moment, which often acted

as a timely reminder—as I would moan about late models or an abusive editor or that a lipstick I was desperately waiting on to shoot hadn't shown up in time—of how lucky I was just to be there, actually getting paid to do what I'd dreamt of for so long.

That day though, I had no complaints, just a mild vomitive feeling in the pit of my stomach. The lift to the studio opened directly onto the set. There, right in front of me, stood 'The Body', Elle Macpherson, being photographed by a handsome, sophisticated-looking man I later learned was Australian photographer Graham Shearer. A beautiful woman, maybe even more impressive than Elle, saw me standing, mouth agape, at the elevator and rushed me inside, thankfully taking the Chanel that had been weighing down my arms and soul as she did. This was Pasha Merk, *Elle*'s French fashion director and Graham's wife. Together, they were sort of Australian fashion royalty. Only a minute earlier, I'd been on planet Earth, having just sidestepped a homeless man to get into the building from a street scattered with syringes, and suddenly I found myself having arrived on Planet Fashion. I was spellbound.

Safely rid of my precious bundle, I lingered awkwardly, not wanting to leave but having absolutely no means to make them want me to stay. I couldn't even offer to make coffee because I'd never made it before and I was pretty sure I'd fuck it up and look like even more of an idiot than I already did. Despite this, I managed to hover uselessly until lunchtime and somehow ended up with a seat at the table. (Publishing back then was a civilised business and this was a sit-down lunch, catered and with actual

metal cutlery, not the Chargrill Charlie's on the run we'd all get used to in years to come.)

I didn't say a thing for the entire meal. I just sat there, silently absorbing every word of every conversation uttered around me. To my ears, so hungry for excitement, these people were like characters out of the Jackie Collins books I sometimes snuck from my mum's bedside table—glamorous and larger than life, with their easy talk of parties, names I recognised from the Sunday paper social section, European vacation spots and fashion labels I'd never dare try to pronounce.

Eventually the shoot resumed. I continued my routine of saying nothing and staring agog. At one point, Elle took off her top and posed with just a pair of white ankle boots held across her naked breasts. The fact that no-one appeared to even notice this seemed to me like the very height of sophistication. How I longed to be the kind of person who could be that indifferent to celebrity boobs! I started practising immediately by very carefully inspecting the ceiling for that entire shot and some of the next, just to be sure.

That is what changed the course of my life: a catered lunch and a set of fashion nipples—although admittedly they were *the* set of fashion nipples.

They're not the worst things I'll ever go on to base a major life decision on.

I CAME, I SAW, I TAPED THE SHOES

FIFTY-FOUR PARK STREET was a dank, charmless building that hadn't been renovated since Frank Packer's day, but to me it was a place where giants walked the halls. The foyer was a parade of wildly stylish, savvy women who looked more like they were heading to a nightclub than to the office. Its corridors smelled like a heady mix of Jean Paul Gaultier Classique perfume and freshly printed ink on paper. I thought it was paradise.

I became a regular work experience person (aka the 'WEP', or even the 'weppie' to the very affectionate/condescending) at any mag that wanted to take me. I plugged away at work experience all through high school. It wasn't just ACP I hung around. Every holidays, I'd book myself in to any publishing house that was lax enough to let me come in without the appropriate liability insurance. Only once I decided to branch out from magazines and apply to the wardrobe department of the TV soap *E Street*.

'Can you sew and pattern-make?' they asked me in the phone interview. 'Yes. Yes I can,' I declared confidently, telling myself

that it wasn't a *complete* lie. I didn't take Textiles as an elective but I didn't do *too* badly in the mandatory Year 7 pyjama project, and I figured once my mum got home and could tell me exactly what pattern-making was, I'd be able to work it out.

I had to take a train and two buses to get to the studio, a two-hour trip each way. I was exhausted when I finally arrived in the wardrobe department, which was bustling and frenetic compared to the relatively calm magazine offices I'd become used to, but I managed to pull myself together and put on a game face. I must have looked a lot more competent than I felt because I was immediately handed a huge pink satin skirt and told to sew a waistband on it by hand. I was shocked. I knew I'd been specifically asked if this was a skill I possessed, but I didn't for a minute think they'd been asking *for an actual reason*. My panic was made worse because the pyjamas had been made on a sewing machine, so the expertise I'd picked up in Year 7 Textiles—including how to thread a bobbin and, well, not much else—was useless in this situation.

I nodded dumbly at the request, too scared to admit I'd lied in the interview. I'd come too far—literally, two hours too far— to admit defeat so quickly. But as I looked at the fabric in my hands, a genuine terror kicked in. The piece of clothing I'd been asked to sew wasn't just any piece of clothing—it was the wedding dress of one of the main characters, for what was being built up to be the episode of the year (I knew this because while I may not have been a capable seamstress, I was actually a fan of the show). Realising that I was in way over my head, I did as I was asked with the only technique I could manage—a horribly

crooked, basic running stitch. It didn't look particularly secure so I went over it twice. This might have been a mistake. By the time I was done, it looked like the wrong side of a cross-stitch done by a hyperactive kindergartener whose mum had forgotten to administer his Ritalin. My heart sank as I inspected my handiwork, a dead giveaway that I was a sham.

Toni Pearen, the actress whose character was getting married on the show, came rushing into wardrobe for a wedding dress fitting between scenes just as I was on my last 'stitch', if that's what you could call it. She hurriedly pulled on my extravaganza and stood in front of the mirror, the entire wardrobe department hovering around her to see how it looked. Her character was known for being partial to hot pants and the skirt had been designed to be completely open at the front, revealing a pair of matching shorts underneath, all topped off by my waistband with its big pink bow. It was a frothy nineties bridal dream, designed by *E Street* wardrobe designer Lizzy Gardiner, who would go on to win an Oscar for her work on *The Adventures of Priscilla, Queen of the Desert*, and who, at that moment, was about to discover that she had a fraud in her midst who thought Janome was a kind of yoghurt. As everyone oohed and ahhed around her, Toni used her hands to gently smooth the skirt. And thus, my inadequate running stitch—already strained by the weight of the fabric—inevitably gave way. The skirt literally fell apart in her hands.

For obvious reasons, for the rest of my time at *E Street* I was relegated to calling the extras to tell them what to wear when they showed up on set the next day, a job even I couldn't fuck up.

'No whites, no stripes, no logos or prints—and please remember, it's always summer in *E Street*!'

~

Television was clearly not for me. I returned to magazines, my spiritual home, where taping the soles of borrowed shoes with masking tape so they wouldn't get ruined during photo shoots was the most technical I would ever have to get.

I continued my work experience routine all through high school, turning up to a different office every term break, dressed in my favourite Esprit, the very definition of eager beaver, ready to perform any menial tasks anyone wanted to pass my way with laser-like, Elle Woods-esque focus and an over-inflated sense of self-importance. I got the coffees, I cleaned the fashion cupboard, I fetched the lunch (always something with sun-dried tomatoes because it was the nineties, but sadly never for me because they cost extra and I was unpaid). I ran the beauty and CD sales, where promotional goodies sent into the mag were sold off cheaply in the office and the money went to charity, among other things (specifically: 20 per cent to charity, 80 per cent to team daiquiris). Digital photography was yet to come along so a huge part of my time involved cutting transparency film strips into tiny squares, putting the best ones into little plastic cases and filing them away in case the magazine ever wanted to use the image again. I lost hours to this monotony, but I loved it all. I did it like my life depended on it. Which, to be honest, it really did, unless I wanted my life to involve the management path at Just Jeans, Miranda Fair.

I'll never be as good at anything in my life as I was at work experience. I went back to the same magazines so often I eventually stopped waiting for the holidays at all and just showed up sometimes after school to catch the last hour or so of the day in my uniform, a teenage *Working Girl* striding into someone else's office with an efficient little pep in my step like I was born to be there. I had the best water-cooler conversation of any sixteen-year-old in Sydney. And eventually even my wardrobe improved, as if by osmosis.

WHEN OPPORTUNITY KNOCKS

THE YEAR 1993 was big for many things: *Jurassic Park*, the Clintons, baby-doll dresses . . . In Australia, it was also a peak era for male models. Generally considered the awkward afterthought of their profession (every man I've ever seen on the runway looks either exactly like he's parodying a *Zoolander* extra or like he's just woken up from a two-decade-long coma and is dumbstruck by life in the modern day), the nineties was their time to shine. The pre-internet omnipotence of the two teen magazines of the era—*Dolly* and *Girlfriend*—made a particular set of young, somewhat unwitting surfing hunks in their early twenties the biggest heart-throbs of our day. British teenagers had Ant and Dec on their walls, the Americans had Coreys Haim and Feldman, and Australian girls worshipped a group of surfing models from Sydney's Northern Beaches.

There was a Jason, a Steven, a Colin and an inordinate number of Nathans, and they could be found on magazine covers, stickers

and posters in bedrooms and Year 12 common rooms all over the country. It was a satisfying kind of reverse objectification—these were boys who did nothing (as far as we knew or cared) but look hot. We didn't know anything about their personalities, they didn't sing or act in *Neighbours* or perform in any way. They were just pure eye candy for an entire generation of teenage girls, like Page 3 Girls but with boardie tan marks and goatees, a bunch of handsome-but-regular dudes who happened to make their livings as toothy accessories to Alison Brahe in photo shoots and being worshipped by fourteen-year-olds nationwide when all their mates were sparky apprentices and landscape gardeners.

I knew who they were, but I didn't have a lot of room in my heart for these local beefcakes. (As far as celebrity crushes went, I'd been in a monogamous relationship with River Phoenix since Year 4. While my friends obsessed over more basic bros like Luke Perry, Mark Wahlberg and the model crew, I smugly assumed that my love for Rio—that's what his mum and I called him—was more real and more special than their silly crushes. Or so I thought, until River died during my HSC year and the school had to postpone the trial 2-unit Maths exam due to *the overwhelming grief of the entire grade.* My deep personal pain got lumped in with everyone else's mass teen hysteria and, frankly, I could not have been more offended.) But this all changed in a hot minute when I met one of them in the flesh, at a party hours away from anywhere I knew while I was trying to escape a 'roided up body-builder on ecstasy and had no way to get home, because this is the sort of adolescent that I was.

It was all my friend Jojo's fault. She was one of those girls who was in a new dramatic relationship with a random older guy every school term. She met them at the gym where they would home in on her vulnerability around the StairMaster. This seemed impressively sophisticated to me at the time, but when I think of her in years to come, the sheer number of creepy older boyfriends she had makes my blood run cold. Jojo didn't have a mum around and the me of the future would very much like to find a DeLorean to go back in time and give that girl a hug and some sage maternal advice.

Jojo wanted me to go to a party with her boyfriend and his brother, both muscle-heads in their late twenties who I'm fairly sure might have been the world's first sentient protein bars. When we got to the boys' house, Jojo and her boyfriend had a fight, as they were wont to do, and decided they didn't want to go to the party anymore so they could stay home and have legally question-able make-up sex instead. The brother tried to talk me into going anyway. He told me how fun it would be and promised to drive me home as soon as I was ready to leave. He was gross, but because I was wearing a new dress I liked, and because I didn't want to stay home on a Saturday night just because Jojo was getting her Dylan and Brenda on, and mostly because I was an idiot, I got into a car with an older man I didn't know and ended up an hour from home in a semi-rural mansion with a lot of very grown-up people doing a lot of very grown-up things. There was a jacuzzi in the living room and the people in it were in various states of undress even though it was winter and freezing. A silver tray was being passed around by a waiter, covered in complimentary lines

of cocaine. Someone told me the house belonged to a 'famous gynaecologist', if there has ever been such a thing, and that a few years earlier, his nanny and her boyfriend had died there after getting so stoned in the sauna that they passed out. Apparently they hadn't been found for several weeks and the sauna had to be ripped out afterwards because of the smell, an idea that made my skin crawl. It was all very far from third-period Geography.

I moved around the room trying to avoid the bodybuilding bro who was attempting to make me take a pill of unknown origin. Eventually I noticed what appeared to be a mirage of normal-looking boys—closer to my age and, notably, not grinding their teeth—in the corner of the kitchen. Their long, scruffy surfer hair and shearling-trimmed denim jackets and jeans, along with the beers they were holding instead of champagne glasses, made them look bizarrely out of place in this room of young, hot women draped off suited older men. I gravitated towards them for the sake of familiarity as much as anything else, and nearly fainted when I realised one of them was Nathan Harvey, king of Sydney's male model heart-throb set and star of the famed de-de-de-Decoré shampoo commercial. We started talking and I tried very hard to pretend I hadn't spent the vast majority of my past two years cutting up transparency sheets of him, clicking them into little white plastic frames and filing them at my fake after-school job.

When my new friend heard about my predicament and realised how far I was from home, he rose to the occasion, uttering that classic Prince Charming line from every childhood fairytale: 'My Valiant's out the front. I'll drive you home.'

And, just like Bonnie and Clyde—if Bonnie and Clyde ever got chased down a suburban gravel driveway by a frothing-at-the-mouth Keto snack—we made our escape.

~

Nathan and I dated for the next few months, as often as he could be bothered to drive the Val from one end of Sydney to the other to see me, which wasn't as often as I would have liked. Being on the arm of a teen heart-throb when you're still a teenager yourself is not something a girl can ever get enough of. He took me to movie premieres and red-carpet events, and once we were photographed together for a full page in the *Daily Telegraph* promoting a charity drive, so obviously I thought I'd fucking made it. The mean girls at school were sick with jealousy, which was lovely. Honestly, it was as close to a Cinderella scenario that a Year 12 student from Sydney's south in 1993 was ever going to get.

Unsurprisingly, the fairytale didn't last. Nathan dumped me over the phone because it was too far to drive to my house to tell me in person. But in a fortuitous turn of events, my school formal—which he kindly still promised to come to, thank god because otherwise *I would have just died*—happened to be scheduled for the same night as *Girlfriend* magazine's Model Search party. Alongside the *Dolly* Model Competition, the *Girlfriend* Model Search was a bizarrely misconceived concept whereby each of the magazines that were supposed to guide the nation's young women thought it was acceptable to ask them send in pictures of themselves to be judged purely on looks alone, leading to the broken spirits of thousands of girls every year who'd been told

their whole lives by well-meaning aunts that they 'could be a model' but who never even got a call back.

Nathan, an aspiring TV presenter, was asked to host the event, but turned it down because he knew it would break my heart even more if he cancelled on me, and also because his mum made him. What happened next was my first experience, though definitely not my last, in how an editor-in-chief will do just about anything to get her way. The *Girlfriend* boss, Kath Brown—a brilliant editor who went on to launch *Red* magazine in the UK— found a clever way around this conundrum. She called me in for a meeting about a job. I thought it was a ruse, a cunning scheme to get me into her office where she would demand I find someone else to take to the formal. I prepared myself to have to show up with a second cousin from Queensland, the only date I'd be able to wrangle at such short notice.

Nonetheless, I prepared for the meeting, which required an outfit that communicated that even though I was still in high school and would need fake ID to come to Friday after-work drinks, I was also unfailingly mature and professional—a mission well beyond the capabilities of my then wardrobe of Vanessa Paradis-inspired flares and crochet waistcoats. Mum took me to Country Road where I chose a teenage interpretation of a Smart Grown-up Lady dress-up costume—a beige wide-legged pant-suit—that I convinced her was 'investment dressing'. I never wore the outfit again, of course, because I had no executive mothers groups to attend, but somehow Kath saw beyond my lamb-dressed-as-mutton look and offered me a job. A real-life job as an editorial assistant, that paid actual money—$12,500 a year, which was

very likely completely illegal but felt like a fortune to me because between all the work experience, my paying shifts at the lotto shop had been few and far between.

I signed on to start at *Girlfriend* three days after my last HSC exam. Of course I had to work at the model party the night of the formal, conveniently freeing Nathan up to MC. It was upsetting, obviously, being dumped by the hottest guy in Australia, but any heartbreak was neutralised by getting my dream job out of it, which seemed like a pretty decent trade to me.

(*Girlfriend* was one of the few magazines I hadn't been interning at and I unwittingly stole the job from the version of me who had been doing work experience there the whole time and was a shoo-in until I showed up with my inconveniently timed formal. All I can hope, to alleviate my guilt, is that after this unfair near miss she decided that publishing was not for her and got a double degree in economics and science instead, and twenty years later is lying around on her private island that she bought with the proceeds of the tech-medical start-up she founded, reading about the demise of the magazine industry thinking, *There but for the grace of God . . .*)

I wore my formal dress to the party, which was probably a bit over the top but I wasn't about to waste it. Mum, a woman who had never had less than three jobs on the go at once to support her family all by herself, took me to a shop in the Strand Arcade and let me choose any dress I wanted, which inexplicably happened to be halter cut with a ruched bust in dark purplish chiffon. I desperately wanted the dress and so I tried not to think about how many hours of cleaning other people's bathrooms Mum had

put in to pay for it. I still have it, tucked away in a box some-where forever, not because of any sentimentality for the dress itself, which can only be described as being the colour of a really hard-core hickie, but as a glaring reminder of how the love of a parent for an unappreciative arsehole really is something to marvel at.

In the end we made it to the formal for the last hour—just enough time for me to get drunk on house sparkling and vomit all over Nathan's lurid purple suit. (Yes, we *matched*—just like the eggplant version of Britney and Justin's double denim.)

I think I got the best of it.

~

Getting the job at *Girlfriend* was my first experience of what I'd come to learn over and over throughout my life: that while the universe doesn't tend to offer us up perfectly wrapped gifts like little blue Tiffany boxes, it will offer us opportunities from time to time if we can put ourselves in a position to grab hold of them. I was a little bit annoyed that all that slaving away at work experience I'd been doing for the preceding three years instead of sucking back on apple bongs at parties like other girls my age wasn't what got me my break in the end, but I also knew it had set me up to be able to leap at my chance when I saw it. It didn't have to happen that way. I'd like to think my hard work would have paid off in the end somehow, but maybe not. And then maybe I would have followed a completely different career path, ending up as a writer of erotic fan fiction or the person who names OPI nail polish colours. That could have been fun. I might

have forgotten all about my teenage love for magazines, the affection fading away over time just like my feelings for River, RIP.

~

Working on a teen magazine as an actual teen was a masterclass in how to not start a career. There was a part of me that was as ambitious and hungry as ever—it only took three months for me to convince my editor to promote me from just editorial assistant to editorial, fashion and beauty assistant, which was mostly just more words in my title but also much more to my liking. And there was another part of me that was still just seventeen, revelling in my newly salaried riches, drunk on my sudden adultness and often just drunk.

It was 1994 and the entertainment industry was flush with grunge money. There were album launches and showcases nearly every night of the week. I went out most nights to work 'functions'—called that even though there wasn't a thing about them that was really necessary to my work or the functioning of it— rolled into the office in the early hours of the morning and slept in the fashion cupboard until other people start arriving at 9 am, at which point I would dress myself in a snazzy Portmans look straight off the styling rack and pop out fresh as a daisy. I could— and often did—party most nights for a month without spending a cent of the $240 I took home a week after tax, which was handy. These were wild, Stoli-fuelled times and I never knew what might happen in the course of an evening on the job. I might have had to chaperone the finalists of the *Girlfriend* model comp in a hotel overnight even though I'd only just turned eighteen myself and

two of them were older than me. I might have smuggled them out to go to a party in Kings Cross that evening and have snuck them back in through the foyer the next morning, making it into the lift only to see their mums and dads (and my boss) walking towards us as the doors closed just in time. My colleagues and I often disappeared from the office for hours to get terrible tattoos like a daisy chain or a sun (I got both; Drew Barrymore has a lot to answer for), or matching belly button rings. (The *Girlfriend* office lived next door to the music magazine *Hot Metal*, and someone who worked across both mags commented that the only difference was that us teen dreams swore more and had more tattoos and piercings between us.) Take That might have requested after an interview that I take them out clubbing and procure them weed to smoke on the dance floor at Mr Goodbar. At a media meet and greet after a show, Anthony Kiedis might have asked to sniff all the female media attendee's armpits, and on a fashion shoot trip I might have organised a whole crew nudie run through the halls of a Coffs Harbour hotel, then be forced by the manager to watch it through barely suppressed giggles on the security-camera footage afterwards. We did it all because you're only young once and, thankfully, there were no such things as camera phones.

LONDON CALLING

I HAD A party pal Cassie, a model who was wild and worldly beyond her twenty years and who had recently moved to London. She called me reverse charges to the *Girlfriend* office all the time, trying to convince me to join her. 'I've got this *incredible* house and *amazing* flatmates. You won't have to pay any rent!' she urged. Cassie was not always the most reliable source and it would probably have been prudent to ask how this could have been the case in one of the world's most expensive cities, but to question such a generous offer just seemed rude. I'd been at *Girlfriend* for almost a year and a half, and I loved my job and being a working woman in my new grown-up world, but a girl couldn't be content interviewing Channel V presenters forever. I was already itchy for the next phase, my next adventure. Could I have gotten it out of my system by grabbing some mates and heading off on a raucous holiday to Bali to make up for the schoolies I'd never made it to because I was already working for the man? Probably, but that would have been too sensible. Much

better to throw caution to the wind, along with everything I'd worked so hard for over the past five years, and resign from my job, fill a backpack I couldn't lift by myself and move to London with £200 in my pocket and only a denim jacket for warmth. (I might have been escaping the suburbs but I had no idea yet how to not dress like I was still there.)

My flight got in late on a Thursday evening. Cassie met me at the airport, gave me a change of clothes to put on in the toilet and—lugging the enormous backpack between us—we headed straight off to the famous gay club, Heaven.

It was my first night in London, the first real night of my adult life. I remember none of it. The next day I woke up in my new digs in the late afternoon. I was on the floor of the living room. It smelled vaguely of cats and fancy cigarettes. In a surprise to myself, I was wearing half a pair of flesh-toned pantihose tied around my chest as a sort of makeshift boob tube. Perhaps more terrifyingly, given that it was only early April in London and already colder than I'd ever experienced in a Sydney winter, my denim jacket—my lone piece of outerwear—was nowhere to be found. It was my first ever experience of a jet-lagged hangover, one of the infamously worst kind of hangovers (right up there with a hangover suffered through while having to look after your own small children which I won't become familiar with until much, much later).

Cassie appeared to be missing in action but one of the 'amazing' flatmates she'd sold me on was there, an older French guy with too many shirt buttons undone and the sort of jewellery that tells you he shouldn't be trusted. He was leering aggressively at my

barely pantihosed areola as I tried to move as quickly as possible, rummaging through my backpack of worldly belongings—which had somehow, astoundingly, made it home with me after the night we've obviously had—for a top that had a hole for a head and was more than eight denier.

He explained that Cassie had gone home with the DJ from the night before and also that if I went out to leave a window open as we didn't have a key. The 'incredible' rent-free house Cas pitched to me so enthusiastically was actually an Earl's Court squat. And with that morsel of information, my jet-lagged hangover became the all-time worst kind of hangover, which is a hangover infused with Big Life Regret.

I never got a chance to ask Cassie what the hell she'd been thinking because she never walked through that Earl's Court door—or, rather, climbed through that Earl's Court window—again. She sent me a message, 1995-style—that is, via an actual person sent on a bike to deliver me a note—from her agency, to let me know that she and the DJ had gone to a festival in Amsterdam and she wasn't sure when they'd be back. I never heard from her again.

A few days later, a posh thirty-something in a Brioni suit who Cassie had been sleeping with pre-DJ—she obviously did not have a type—came around looking for her. He saw my predicament and felt sorry for me, or perhaps less altruistically, he saw an opportunity with a helpless, vulnerable, underdressed Australian. He offered me a tiny attic room in his Fulham townhouse, available in a week once he kicked out a freeloading friend. I'd have to pay rent and remember to keep the bedroom locked for my

own safety at all times, but at least living there I could enter through the front door.

That day I also got a job as a hostess at the Sports Cafe in Piccadilly which was just opening. I celebrated this double win by going to Portobello Road and spending what was left of my £200 on a leather jacket. I could afford to be blasé about my cashflow because I was fairly confident that my time in London wouldn't last the month.

~

I'd never had a hospitality job before and I was sensationally awful at it. The job I'd been hired for was to stand at the entrance of the venue and greet the customers as they came in with a bored, 'Hi, welcome to the Sports Cafe, how many in your party?' For this, I got two paid days of training, most of which was spent being warned not to flirt or get physical with the clientele, something none of us had any intention of paying heed to. The place was essentially a backpacker brothel that just happened to serve three different kinds of buffalo wings.

On opening night, they packed the place full of sports celebrities, but having so recently arrived and without the slightest fluency in sports even in my native language, it all went over my head. I flirted with a boy—cheeky, laddish and with a wide grin and a 'Sarf London' accent that my fresh-off-the-boat ears found highly exotic—who told me he played football, and I'd watched enough *Grange Hill* to know that meant soccer. We had a highly forbidden pash in the cloakroom at the end of the night, after which he offered to drop me off to the Earl's Court hovel where

I was unfortunately still living. From the safety of the black cab, he looked up at the house—the smashed windows, the general air of misery and aroma of yesterday's Nando's hanging around it—and thought better about coming in. If only I had done the same on my first night. Instead, he invited me to watch him play football on the weekend. *Weird first date*, I thought, putting it down to cultural differences, but I convinced a girl from my new work (an equally clueless Kiwi import) to come and stand on the sidelines of some football field and watch a bunch of grown men play weekend sport because I had nothing else to do anyway.

In the meantime, I moved into the Fulham townhouse, and when the day for the date came it turned out that we could walk from my new digs to the address I'd been given. We battled our way down the street with what felt like thousands of drunk people dressed in blue and white. I was still confused when we followed the herd into an enormous stadium and picked up our tickets from the ticket office. It wasn't until we were being guided to killer seats that I realised I wasn't there to watch a suburban footy match and that there were 30,000 other people on my date with me.

The roar of the crowd as the boy from the Sports Cafe and his Chelsea Football Club teammates ran out onto the pitch was deafening. He was a defender but that day he happened to score a goal which, for a nineteen-year-old antipodean new arrival, was a real first-date pants-dropper.

There was a note with the tickets explaining where to meet after the game, in a place mysteriously just called 'the bar'. The players' bar is essentially the football version of a green room—a private

and nondescript but heavily guarded box hidden in the depths of the stadium where all the players' family and friends wait for them to finish up their homoerotic group ice bath and meet up after the game. Chelsea was about a year away from the revival that would make them the glamour club they once were again, but even that day the bar was still packed to the rafters with celebrities. I felt like I was in the nineties London version of those weird art prints that show Marilyn Monroe, James Dean, Humphrey Bogart and Elvis together playing pool—but with Damon Albarn from Blur, Baby Spice and Yasmin Le Bon drinking vodka, lime and sodas instead.

The boy and I were immediately inseparable. He was kind and funny, and also sweetly conservative and naive. He didn't really drink or party because of football so we fell into an instant sort of middle age. I didn't mind. I was done with adventures after my wild first year out of school and still traumatised by my move to London. Being with him gave me an immediate anchor, a family on the other side of the world and—being right in the middle of the Cool Britannia era—all the Dolce & Gabbana white tank top and knicker sets to wear with my low-slung cargo pants that I could handle.

I quickly tired of the Sports Cafe gig where even the fact that the phone at the hostess desk could call international—something I took full advantage of at least three out of the four hours of every shift—was no consolation for the relentless bullying by the waitresses (who were probably rightfully pissed that I spent most of my time on the phone to Australia) and the roving hands of patrons who reeked of lager and giant onion rings. I quit and

moved in with the boy, using my newly freed-up time to get back to my work experience roots—albeit this time as a much smaller fish in a much bigger pond—in the hope of eventually getting another job in magazines. When I didn't have an internship to go to, I went with him to training and sat in the car for hours reading magazines to pass the time. This was pathetic, but even more pathetically, I wasn't alone. The club had recently signed a bunch of international players. None of the girlfriends knew each other, none seemed to have anything to do that wasn't Harvey Nichols-related and none had any inclination to bond. The carpark each day was a line-up of brand-new BMWs and the odd Ferrari occupied by bored, imported girlfriends, all flicking through different international editions of *Vogue*.

I missed having a proper job, I missed my friends and I missed having a life outside my boyfriend. I was also homesick. Once my aunt sent me a care package full of Twisties and Nougat Honey Logs and a cassette tape called *Sounds of Jervis Bay*. After it arrived in the post I cranked up the underfloor heating, laid out on a towel in my bikini and sunglasses, slathered myself in coconut oil and 'sunbaked' for a solid three hours to the sound of bird calls, waves crashing and gentle wind chimes, only facing the reality of downtown Beckenham whenever the tape ran out and I had to get up to turn it over.

It was the mid-nineties. People weren't such achievers. There were no socials to curate a perfect life for, no such thing as a side hustle. We hadn't even heard of the terms 'optimisation' or 'self-improvement'. In this world, sunbaking on my living room floor seemed like a perfectly reasonable way to pass the time.

When I eventually did get a job—as the beauty assistant at the *Clothes Show* magazine, a print spin-off of a wildly successful and long-running BBC Sunday evening fashion TV show—it couldn't have come quick enough for either my mental health or my dignity.

THE VERY WORST WAG THAT EVER THERE WAS

FRANGIPANIS EVERYWHERE. A NEW bikini every day. Burgers with beetroot, pineapple and barbecue sauce, chips with more chicken salt than potato, and chocolate milkshakes from takeaway shops in tiny coastal towns that seem frozen in time. Beach towels hanging from a Hills hoist. The glare of the light, the flicking of flies, the taste of salt in the air. Dozing off to the hum of cicadas and the rhythm of frogs. The lazy drift of an aimless, humid afternoon and tossing through restless nights when it's too hot to sleep. The whirr of a fan over your bed. Smoke in the air. The smell of Reef Oil. That torturous decision between a Calippo or a Paddle Pop or a Golden Gaytime or a Weis Bar. Reading a magazine on the beach and taking most of the sand home in its pages. Peeling prawns still wrapped in white paper around the table. Mango dripping down your chin. Backyard barbecues that turn into all-night parties that turn into head-aches I'd sooner forget that can only be cured by dunking my head in the ocean. The burn of hot bitumen under bare feet.

That feeling in the air when it's about to storm. Parties at the surf club. The sounds of Marco Polo from a neighbour's pool, an uncle snoring in front of TV cricket . . .

The entire time I lived in London, I was homesick. Even after I got a job I was homesick. Even after I made friends of my own and got a life outside of my sweet, patient boyfriend, I was homesick. When I was sitting on the tube going to work in the dark, then sitting on the tube coming home in the dark, I'd let myself drift off and dream of the Sydney summer, which I'd romanticised to epic proportions in my head. I pictured it in nostalgic, rose-coloured *Puberty Blues*-like flashes, never breaking out of the reverie even when someone shouted 'Can you move down, please?!' in a carriage with no space, leading me and everyone else to dutifully shuffle around in a sad, aimless circle.

By this time, I knew what the offside rule was about, though that didn't make me any more interested in the game. I sat in the wives' box every second Saturday with a novel—something like *The Secret History* which I hoped would make it clear to anyone paying attention that this football malarky was not my *thing*— and I felt homesick.

Each year I returned to Australia from London just before Christmas and stayed as long as I possibly could. I missed the jacarandas by leaving it so late, missed the thrill of touching down into a landscape dotted with the vibrant purple patches that herald the coming of summer in Sydney, but that was the pay-off for warmer water and longer days. My timing gave me the strongest hit of Sydney summer before I headed back to the dreariness of a London winter. It filled my quota so I could look

past all the pasty shirtless bodies on Clapham Common during the three sunny days in June before my next trip home.

Despite a near-constant yearning for sunshine and chips with chicken salt, it was hard to not fall in love with nineties-era London. I had a job that impressed my nanna's friends at home ('Ooh, the BBC! Ask her if she knows Hyacinth Bucket!') and friends of my own. Even football got interesting. Chelsea started buying in some star European players who increased the excitement around the club. WAGs became a thing. Each week, more celebrities filled the players' bar, a never-ending stream of ageing rock stars, children's TV presenters and all the remaining Spice Girls.

In 1997, the club made the FA Cup Final. Initially, this meant absolutely nothing to me, but even for the most nonplussed, unworthy of WAGs, it was impossible to resist getting caught up in the excitement—and not just because I bought myself a new Prada nylon tote bag for the occasion, although mostly that.

The morning of the game, there was a breakfast held at Stamford Bridge, the Chelsea home ground, for players and their partners. Making the FA Cup Final is a Proper Big Deal for any football player. The energy was palpable and even I started to get nerves, despite the fact that the result meant nothing to me (I already had my Prada bag). The players were whisked away on one bus to Wembley while the partners—Alberta Ferretti-clad butterflies with rich-girl blow-dries and limbs glimmering with Nars Body Oil—were put on another. The crowd was wild and as our bus pulled in, it swarmed, chanting and singing the both catchy and awful new club song that had been written especially

for the day by the eighties band Madness. Each player was given just two tickets and I was seated with my boyfriend's dad, a mad football fan who spent the entire game crying into the hot dogs he bought us that he was too nervous and I was too self-conscious to eat, barely believing he was watching his son play at Wembley in the FA Cup Final. It was the first game I'd ever been to where my book, which I'd brought along mostly out of habit, stayed well and truly in my bag.

Chelsea won. The mood in the players' bar was one of testosterone-fuelled hysteria. The English players were chanting and letting the Italian players kiss them hard on the mouth and they were all sobbing, down to the very last boot boy. After a couple of hours of crying and hugging and opening £1000 bottles of Krug like it was Fanta, we were taken on coaches to the Savoy Hotel where we were given suites by the club and went on to party long into the night at a gala dinner that I can only imagine would have been massively depressing if they'd lost. I danced—along with all the other wives and girlfriends—with superstar special guest Pelé and we all took turns posing with the lid of the cup trophy on our heads. In the morning we dragged our happy, hungover selves onto an open-top bus for the victory tickertape parade, which wound through the streets of London from the Savoy back to Stamford Bridge, as screaming people lined the streets and did crazy things like hand babies up to the players—atop a *moving bus*—to sign, flash their bums and/or boobs and yell at us from upstairs flats along the route to watch them having sex in their windows. I felt a bit like I was in a very strange dream—a surreal amalgamation of the 'Wheels on the

Bus' and *Benny Hill*. The front page of the *Sunday Times* the next day featured a huge picture of us all on the bus. We were pretty squished so you have to really squint to see that it's me with the oversized sunglasses atop a brassy highlighted Rachel cut, but I can assure you that it is.

The FA Cup Final was more than just an excellent knees-up. My boyfriend was at the end of his contract with Chelsea, which meant he could move to an international club without one of those crazy, multimillion-dollar transfer fees European soccer is famous for. Because of this, all eyes were on him throughout the game and afterwards we waited for the offers to come in. I'd been convinced to give up my job for an international adventure a second time with a Tiffany engagement ring and the promise of endless sunshine—although I didn't need much convincing because after a couple of years in London, my underfloor heat sunbaking days were done. Contracts came in from Bordeaux in France and Benfica in Portugal. I looked them both up on a map and chose Benfica because of its proximity to the beach.

Our departure came quickly, the night after my twenty-first birthday party at Brown's nightclub. And just like that, I became a full-time Euro WAG, albeit a somewhat lacklustre one. Sky Sports accompanied us on the plane to Lisbon and filmed a segment with my boyfriend pretending to sleep on my shoulder during the flight. For this fifteen minutes of fame, I chose to wear jeans and a shiny shrunken purple T-shirt from Topshop. New Prada tote and Tiffany sparkler aside, we were too naive to have any idea what to do with all that insane soccer money. Most of the time I was just stoked to not have to worry about the prices at

Wax Lyrical, the London chain that sold an astounding variety of colourful floating flower candles. Between an endless supply of those and the three different colours of Casio Baby-G watch in my possession, I was as bougie as I knew how to be.

~

Lisbon was a culture shock. Benfica FC was a behemoth, with fans numbering half the population of the entire country. *Fans* wasn't quite the right word, though. In the eye of the Benfica supporters, the players worked for *them* and so, like angry bosses, they regularly accosted us in the street, yelling at both of us if they thought he should be training or at home resting instead of shopping or out having dinner in a restaurant—something we had no choice in because my culinary skills were so limited that sometimes when people came to our house for dinner, my boyfriend would suddenly start taking everyone's pizza delivery order halfway through entrees, as though what I'd cooked was just a joke amuse-bouche and we'd planned it that way all along.

Adding to my cultural whiplash was the fact that I'd signed a contract with the club myself. What this meant, other than not having my own job to occupy me, was that all the conduct rules that applied to the players also applied to me in a kind of warped variation of 'happy wife, happy life'.

In London, the team had trained for a few hours each day. At Benfica, they trained for twice as long, so I had a lot of time at home to be alone with my thoughts, which as it turned out were not all that great company. If a big game was coming up and the club wanted an extra training session out of the players,

they would send the expat WAGs away on an enforced group shopping trip to somewhere we couldn't get in the way—like Milan or Brussels—where we stomped in and out of change rooms in strappy heels and aggressive blow-dries, each wanting to be anywhere else but there with the others.

Portuguese television was all dubbed, so I relied on VHS box sets of *Friends*, *Seinfeld* and *The X-Files* sent over by family and friends from London for entertainment. One of the few available cable news networks started showing the trial of the UK 'Nanny Killer' case live and I would nearly cry when court adjourned at the end of each day, not because I was so emotionally invested in the case but because I didn't know what I'd do with myself once it was over. I had friends come to stay from London and Sydney as often as I could and eventually became close to some of the other expat players' partners, but instead of using the time to become excellent at tennis or learn to be a cordon bleu cook or pick up a language—Portuguese, perhaps?—I mostly just ate custard tarts. I'd eat them incredibly slowly to really stretch out the time and make this one thing I had planned in my day last as long as possible. To this day, I only have to smell the combination of eggs and sugar to experience an instant wave of hopeless ennui.

I started to feel caged. Our contract with the club specified that we couldn't be out past midnight on any given night or his salary would be docked £100 per minute—for each of us. One night, we rolled in just before 1 am after a rousing dinner with some friends from London who were staying with us. It earned us an immediate £10,000 fine. With the exchange rate,

that was more than I earned my entire first year at *Girlfriend*. There was no getting away with anything because we lived in a compound where the security guards were paid off by the club, who also held our passports. I had to ask permission to go home to visit my family or to go back to London to see friends, and it was never viewed favourably because—to their thinking—a player whose significant other was out of town would be unhappy and not perform as well on the pitch. I wanted to tell them that a player whose significant other was a cranky bitch because she was stuck in her sunny, elegant Euro jail-home with seventeen and a half hours to go until her next appointment with a custard tart could make a player just as unhappy but, alas, I didn't speak the language.

After about a year or so of this privileged inertia, I flew back to Australia to organise our wedding—despite marriage, as a rule, not being something the kind of twenty-two-year-old I was should be doing anyway. Not long after I arrived, I realised that I really didn't want to go back. I loved my boyfriend, or thought I did, but I didn't love WAG life. I just wasn't cut out for it. My two-week trip home was extended to three weeks, then four, then six. He was too nice, too polite and too English to demand that I return at any point, but eventually I got a call from someone at Adidas, a sponsor, who told me in no uncertain terms to haul my sorry arse back there, *imediatamente*.

I cried the whole way back to Lisbon, no idea of what I was going to do. After all those years of wanting *more*, I'd finally got it: a wonderful fiancé, a glamorous (on the surface anyway) life-style, enough money to fill an Olympic-sized swimming pool

with floating flower candles—but it still wasn't enough. I couldn't help but wonder if anything ever would be.

Just a few weeks later, nearly four years after my denim jacket and I first showed up in London, I called off our engagement and flew back to Australia for good. I felt pretty sure that I was making the stupidest decision of my life but, tellingly, I didn't cry at all on the way home. I landed having realised the truth: I still wanted more, a bigger life, but I needed it to be all my own, on my terms. Piggybacking off the back of someone else's big life would never be enough.

I left not speaking a word of Portuguese or knowing a thing about soccer or anything much else, but to this day I can still recite every word of every episode from every season of *Friends*, so I guess that's something.

THE BEAUTY EDITOR MYTH

I DIDN'T GO to university, and because of that there were things I missed out on—a formal education for one, but also a tie-dye phase, a nostalgic affection for Jägermeister, a wide repertoire of ways to dress up Mi Goreng instant noodles, HECS debt . . . Instead, I was a beauty editor throughout most of my formative years so beauty became my university, just with champagne breakfasts instead of beer pong.

Life as a beauty editor was sweet, or at least it was then. My life was a daily cycle of beautiful lunches, fabulous events, extravagant presents, exotic trips, PRs trying to outdo each other with money-can't-buy experiences, and endless spa treatments—all in the name of trying to get me and my peers to write about a product that was being launched in whatever magazine or newspaper we happened to work for. One time, I took home a one-carat diamond lucky door prize from a Maybelline lip gloss launch, the message being that this particular gloss could make lips sparkle just like diamonds, obviously. Another time I left a

Sunsilk shampoo event with a Louis Vuitton suitcase. I'm not sure what the message was in that case—maybe to remind me how much this particular shampoo could make you look really, really expensive? The connection's not incredibly clear, but it wasn't like I was complaining.

Despite the cushiness—and we are talking some next-level cush—being a beauty editor was a highly respected position on a magazine because most advertising came from the world of beauty, so you were a vital cog in the business of publishing. You were also the genteel overlord of the infamous magazine 'beauty cupboard', which is essentially the entire ground floor of David Jones crammed into labelled baskets in a small closet with no air . . . but who needs air when you have endless Tom Ford? This position of power made you everyone on the magazine's best friend.

But the real friends in beauty were to be made from the magazines you were meant to be competing with. Beauty editors are, by and large, some of the loveliest humans you could ever hope to meet. It's almost a prerequisite for the job. You have to be a solid writer, a dab hand with a lipstick swatch and have an exceptional ability to stay interested and keep smiling through endless PowerPoint presentations of cross-sections of epidermis. It requires a genuinely patient and sweet nature to be able to spend such a huge proportion of your time socialising with strangers and gushing over new eyeshadow shades without wanting to die a little bit inside. That was the hardest part for me, all that professional niceness. I found it exhausting. (It will come as a real relief when I eventually get the top job and don't need to

smile so much that my jaw hurts at the end of the day and can also let out as many f-bombs as I please.)

While it's quite easy to be a mediocre beauty editor—as long as the advertisers like you and your name sits under the right masthead, you can get away with essentially recycling the same stories year after year (sun care in January, perfumes in May and December, hair in June, make-up in September), just replacing the products and expert quotes for fresh ones—being a great beauty ed is more challenging. It takes real talent to make magic out of a 200-word piece on yet another hyaluronic acid serum. You have to really *care*. I love beauty products as much as the next woman, but I always felt something of a fraud in the role. There's a long list of things I am deeply interested in—American politics, international street food trends, whatever Gwyneth Paltrow is doing—but skincare delivery systems has never really been one of them.

However, because of all the loveliness, it was an amazing place to spend my twenties. I made lots of best friends from my fellow beauty editors—because if you can't make lifelong BFFs on the beauty circuit, you're very likely shrivelled up inside. Beauty editors spent more time with each other than we did with our own teams, and sometimes even our partners or families. We ate the majority of our meals together in the city's best restaurants and were plied with copious amounts of Veuve Clicquot—not that a good beauty editor would *ever* get drunk—on semi-regular adult sleepovers in chic countryside hotels. Because the beauty companies' efforts to impress could be so outlandish (launch a moisturiser on the top of the Sydney Harbour Bridge! Travel to India to learn about hair extensions!), the beauty squad's shared

experiences created a bond kind of like that of contestants on *The Bachelor*—built on better, more highly produced memories than you could have ever found the time or money to have with your other, non-beauty friends (but without the bit about having to be part of a harem in a hot girl jail). I journeyed on countless seaplanes with my fellow beauty editors, went to many, many health retreats with them and have not just one but multiple stars named after ourselves sitting together in the sky (stars winning the award for most popular 'unique' press gift for a couple of years, a mantle also held at various times by Tiffany keyrings, monogrammed bathrobes, French market baskets and smash cakes with product inside). It was a strangely decadent way to live considering that the role of beauty editor has never been a particularly well-paid one. Realising you weren't going to make the rent that week on the magnolia-painted single room in your share apartment from the seat of a helicopter taking off from a private Fijian island while someone gives you a foot massage using a new designer-scented foot cream is surely a juxtaposition unique to that job and that job alone.

But I wasn't in it for the good times or even for the products and the perks—I was in it because it was the pathway to editor-in-chief lyfe. I just *stayed* for the good times. It's easy to get stuck, when your rut is such a pleasant one. In the end, I spent fourteen years writing beauty, which truly is too many 'Summer Body Specials' for any brain to resist atrophying.

As a beauty writer, I was a classic case of 'do as I say, not as I do'. For example, I never washed my face at night, not even when it was covered in make-up, not ever. It was a blatant flouting of

every 'Beauty Rules' story I'd ever put my name to, which were numerous.

There were occasions where I wouldn't even recommend doing as I said, let alone what I did. For example, I wrote about permanent laser hair removal in every November issue for years (it being the only month on the calendar when the magazine gods deem everyone in the country suddenly needs hairless legs) prior to actually having it done myself. I wrote about it the way that it was described to me by the experts I interviewed, the same way that every beauty editor wrote about it: 'It feels like an elastic band lightly snapping against the skin.'

I wrote that sentence, or something to that effect (but nah, probably exactly that sentence), five or six times before I could report from actual experience. And maybe I didn't think the words through properly the many times I typed them, but I didn't think that it sounded too painful. Just the opposite in fact: I thought it had a fun, office supplies sound to it.

I'll never know how many women were encouraged to have their body hair permanently zapped off as a result of my writing this phrase so flippantly (probably quite a few because in those days people still actually read magazines) but I know that I owe them all an enormous apology because when I finally got it done myself, on my actual person, I realised that I had vastly undersold the whole deal. The truth was that, back then in its early years, laser hair removal *hurt*. It hurt like hell. It felt like an elastic band snapping lightly against the skin if the elastic band was made of poisonous thumbtacks and the snapping was happening in a BDSM club by a person in a gimp mask wearing gloves that were

on fire as they did it. And I say this as a woman who has been in labour for a total of 133 of the hours of my life and has lived through a post-baby hemorrhoidectomy, which I know for a fact is the worst pain that a human being can ever experience. After I had my bits lasered, I contemplated taking out a full-page ad in the newspaper to apologise for all the lies I'd told. And to add salt to the wound: *it wasn't even really permanent.*

For anyone who suffered in any way as a result of my irresponsible reporting, I can only hope that their eternally(ish) silky smooth labia was worth all the trauma.

~

These days, saying that you were once a beauty editor is akin to saying that once upon a time you were a stegosaurus, or a BlackBerry. Beauty editors are, by and large, heading for extinction—at least here in Australia, now that there are so few magazines left. They've been phased out by an industry that quickly learned that videos made by clones of Kylie Jenner were better than print for selling the astonishing amounts of make-up required to complete the complicated contouring and brow-defining techniques necessary for living your life almost exclusively on Instagram. As a result, the brands moved the money that was keeping most magazines afloat out of publishing and into social media and YouTube swiftly and brutally. As well as haemorrhaging copy sales in a world that was becoming more and more digitally-focused, the sudden drying up of beauty industry investment was one of the key elements in the death of print. What was once the backbone of a magazine's advertising revenue

disappeared faster than you could say 'smoky eye tutorial', and from then on, our world was never the same.

The OTT extravagance I experienced in my beauty editor years is still around today to some degree, but now the launch budgets need to be shared among print press (what's left of it) and all the lifestyle websites, Instagram stars, YouTube channels and various species of blogger (beauty/personal style/mummy, etc.) whose audiences the brand wants to reach as well. It's a bit like going from being an only child to the older sister of triplets. Sure, your parents still love you, but suddenly there's only so much attention and pony club money to go around.

~

It's always the transitional period that's the hardest. In the early days of this merging of worlds, a beauty company held an event that involved flying both old-school (print) and new-school (digital) beauty media from Sydney to Melbourne. As one of the most experienced and established beauty journalists in the country took her seat, she heard a vlogger behind her scoff scornfully to her friend, 'Why do they even invite traditional media? No-one these days even wants that look.' In that moment, my friend realised that the beauty influencer 'look'—the contoured cheeks, the blatant filler, the extreme lashes—had become so ubiquitous that by resisting it, it was now she who was considered to have a 'look'—and also that it was maybe time to move on.

A few years later, I went to the launch of a luxury make-up range. There were all the usual canapés and themed cocktails and cute little Instagram-friendly selfie stations set up in every

corner. But there was one key difference. For the very first time that I'd ever noticed, digital beauty influencers outnumbered print beauty editors on the guest list by a mile, and for the first time since I started coming to these events as a nervous seventeen-year-old, I felt like a fish out of water. With their hyper-real skin, sharply defined brows, lasered hairlines and plumped lips, the influencers looked like a different kind of human altogether—a more perfect, but also more homogeneous, new breed. Homo Kardashianus. I wondered what they saw when they looked at me, as always minimally made up and messily air-dried. I considered my look natural, but to them, I'm pretty sure I must have looked half-baked, as though I'd just rolled out of bed, and—having clearly skipped my three brow products and fourteen-step Korean skincare routine—like I hadn't even tried. But you know, I had tried, it's just that by this stage I had bigger fish to fry. My knees had been looking old lately for one, plus I seemed to spend an inordinate amount of time pulling out hairs from my person: grey ones from my head, rogue spiky ones from the mole above the corner of my mouth. I have a pure white one that grows on my face, just underneath my eye, and is often the length of my thumbnail before I notice it. I've heard that one way to conquer your fears is to name them, so I call him Ian. Fuck off, Ian.

But I couldn't explain this to them, these influencers with their young knees and hair in all the right places. So instead I stared at them, trying to work out where their actual skin was, and they avoided me, in case any of my human imperfection should rub off on them. Eventually, I went home and tidied up my brows. I couldn't help myself. The pressure was too much.

LIKE A BOSS

AFTER SO MANY years in publishing, I've had all the kinds of bosses it's possible to have. I've had the boss who was so charismatic that I and everyone else who worked for her would find ourselves subconsciously trying to become her, adopting her speech patterns and mannerisms, gradually letting her style—all sequins and colourful prints and costume jewellery—infiltrate our wardrobes. She ruled an entire generation of ambitious wannabe magazine editors, her very own cult of clever cool-girls, the best and brightest of an industry made up almost exclusively of bests and brightests. In an effort to impress her, we'd all race to get into the office on Monday mornings and be first to fire off an email of ideas gleaned from the Sunday papers over the weekend. (What a quaint sentence. This was back in the days before smart phones, when work ended on Friday afternoon and started back on Monday, and the Sunday papers were not only purchased and read but were also our main sources of inspiration. How ye olde-worlde.) It was ideation as a competitive sport, and I'd often break out

in an actual speed-typing sweat in my effort to be the first into her inbox.

With a single word or a pointed silence, she could make you feel like the shiniest person in the universe—or send your burgeoning ego crashing back down to earth. I learned so much from her on how to spot talent and how to build a culture, but more than anything she sharpened my mind. We might have looked bright and sparkly, the girls who were her disciples, but we were bright and sparkly *like a fox*.

I've had the boss who'd scream to me from her office twenty metres down the corridor, making me rush to her in a mad panic only to have her ask something completely innocuous—like 'What day are you shooting again next week?'—that could have very easily been communicated via a civilised inter-office phone call. It really played havoc on the nerves. She was very important and very busy and, not wanting to waste a minute of her own time, she'd demand that a planning discussion continue on her way to the loo, where I'd find myself selling a story idea through a cubicle door, trying not to let the sound of her pee tinkling against the bowl distract me from my pitch. Or she'd offer to drive me home so we could discuss my features plan in the car, but would then just obliviously drive me to her house in the complete opposite direction—leaving me unceremoniously in her driveway where I'd then have to walk twenty-five minutes to a main road to find a cab in heels, laden down with bags of beauty products to take to a shoot the next day. Sometimes, as one of the lone single girls in the office, I'd be lucky enough to be set up with one of her husband's friends unasked, which would inevitably lead her to

get annoyed with me when I didn't want a second date, and she was always yelling at me for putting 'too much personality' into the editor's letters the writers on the team would have to take turns ghostwriting for her from incomprehensible notes scratched onto scraps of hotel paper and the back of cab receipts. Trying to write in the warm, authentically friendly tone of someone who rarely spoke to me in anything less than an irritated yell was one of the greatest creative challenges I've ever faced.

Yet I loved working for her, eccentricities and all. Maybe it was Stockholm syndrome, but the picture she painted so vividly for us, her minions, was that *she* was the centre of the world and so, as her satellites, we thought *we* were the centre of the world. Or at least part of something vitally important. And while I didn't appreciate it at the time, fear is a great teacher. I'm yet to meet anyone more efficient or professional than those of us who worked in that office. Emotional scars fade, but good training lasts a lifetime. (Well, actually, they both last a lifetime, but at least the good training can help pay for your therapy.)

I've had the boss who it was always best to approach with a fresh manicure if you needed to get anything signed off. It was the not-so-secret weapon of everyone who worked for her. When taking her something important for approval, like, say, a cover or a proposed salary for a new staff member, everyone knew that shiny new nails were the key to getting what you wanted. On deadline day, you'd more likely than not find me bolting out to USA Nails for a mani just so I could guarantee we'd get to print. It may have seemed ridiculous but it was a foolproof strategy. As you'd walk into her office, her eyes would

be drawn like a bower bird's to your hands, which would lead to twenty minutes of chatter about various beauty products and trends, after which she'd realise she had somewhere else much more important to be and hurriedly start to usher you out as you quickly proposed whatever it was you were there for in the first place and got an almost guaranteed 'Yes, darling, fabulous, darling' while being pushed out the door. This exchange, I soon learned, was a performance, a masterclass in how to be a wolf in sheep's clothing. After years at the top of her game, she knew that the best management skill you can have is to know how to hire good people and then get out of their way. She trusted her editors to know their audiences better than she did and to make their own decisions—as long as you were performing, she didn't feel the need to step in and make them for you. But when you started making decisions that didn't work, you knew about it, whether your fingers were painted in Chanel Particulière or not.

I've had the boss who ended every meeting with a cuddle. There you'd be, having decided on the careful placement of a L'Oréal ad and going over your taxi expenditure and, before you knew it, you'd find your face buried in her perfect blonde coiffure as she pulled you in for a full-body embrace. I've had the boss whose wine I had to secretly water down halfway through every function lest she get drunk and start feeling up the waitstaff. I've had the micromanaging boss whose need for absolute control was never sated unless I carbon-copied her on every single email I sent, leading me to once automatically cc her on an email to my husband reminding him that I was ovulating that night. Then there was the boss who'd creep around my desk when I was

a beauty editor, opening and taking for herself any little goodies that had been sent my way. Once, she half-ate a cake a friend had sent to me on my birthday. I assume she thought it was a press gift, but I can't be sure. All I know is that I came back to my desk after a meeting to a cardboard cake box that had been ripped open through the middle (sticky tape apparently being too hard to peel) and a New York cheesecake missing a chunk that appeared to have been gouged out by hand, topped with a post-it note that just said 'Sorry—starving!'. Later, after someone told her how upset I was about the situation, she sent me an email to say that she really was sorry but also that 'it actually wasn't even that good'.

~

When I finally became a boss myself, I had no idea what sort I'd be. I suspected I had it in me to be both a mother hen and Machiavellian, to reign with terror and also with homemade baked goods. Until then, my only experience as a boss had been starting a kids edition of *Shop Til You Drop* magazine—hereafter referred to as just *Shop*, because *Shop Til You Drop* falls too well into that long line of nonsensical Park Street magazine names, like *Cleo* (after Cleopatra), *The Australian Women's Weekly* (which is published monthly) and *Woman's Day* (which is published weekly) and *Dolly* (just, no). In keeping with the shit name tradition, the magazine was called *Shop 4 Kids*. I was given the project because I was the only person on the team with a child, and it was so insignificant within the company that I wasn't ever asked to consult a single research team or focus group and there was

never any talk of demographics or what types of mothers might buy a fashion magazine for children. If there had been, I think the product we would have ended up with would have been quite different. The magazine that we made, so under the radar, instead developed a cult following for its pages full of fashion shoots of baby skinny jeans and kids picking their noses, and tips on how to dress your children like Kate Hudson's. We did such a thorough job of squeezing chubby little legs into immovable tight denim that, truly, if in twenty years' time we learn that an entire generation of people born circa 2006 in Bondi and St Kilda are known to suffer from chronic hip flexor issues, I will only be able to blame myself.

Shop 4 Kids was made by just myself, a designer and an assistant, working out of an office that was really an oversized stationery cupboard, so I wasn't really the boss of anything except where to put the printer paper if we needed to make room for someone to come in for a meeting. My chance to see what boss stuff I was made of didn't really come until I was offered the role as editor of the main, grown-up version of *Shop*.

~

I'd dreamt of being an editor for so long that there was no way finally becoming one could have been anything other than an anticlimax, not dissimilar to when I finally picked up my former primary school crush Ryan Warren in a nightclub in my twenties and realised after I got him home that now I was no longer so impressed by his making it to regional long jump, he was just like any other sweaty guy you met in a nightclub, and maybe

even more depressing because of the build-up. I'd been picturing some sort of ceremonial anointing, being handed a mint green velvet-lined box, perhaps, containing a special key to the building. A Marauder's Map, with tiny little editor and publisher illustrations moving about the floors, or an ancient papyrus book from the 1970s filled with all of the company secrets only Very Important Employees were allowed to know, along with an annotated guide to all of the rumoured hidden passageways built for Kerry Packer's mistresses.

(It had been a year and a half since Kerry had died, taking with him both the prestige that came from working at a place of Australian folklore *and* the famous ACP staff Christmas hampers he gave to everyone each year. James couldn't cut us off his Santa list quick enough and it was a move the collective staff body never quite got over. It's hard to retain iconic status and keep morale high in a place of dwindling profits, a revolving circus of David Brent-esque CEOs, relentless rounds of redundancies and a workforce that still bitterly mourned the loss of their symbolic basket of ham, smoked salmon and a delicious variety of nonperishables every December.)

I got no mythical key, no access to the mistress tunnels. Just a perfunctory HR negotiation, an email that told me I'd need to continue to use my old work ID card—disappointing, as I'd last had the photo taken during an ill-advised Gwen Stefani heavy fringe stage and it was not a look I felt confident being on record as my official 'editor' face—and a contract that could have been signing me up to work part-time at the local McDonald's for all the gravitas it contained.

~

My boss style turned out to be influenced by one primary factor: I was a mother. I'd fallen pregnant with my first baby when I was twenty-seven and working as the deputy editor on *Dolly* magazine. I was only three months into the job when it happened and not eligible for any maternity leave, so I resigned a few months into the pregnancy so I could establish myself as a freelance writer before the baby came. Twenty-one months after the birth of Milo came Iggy, and two years after that I landed my first editorship. If I was ever worried about whether I was qualified for the top job, I needn't have been. Parenting is a perfect primer for management. There's even an actual management theory called VUCA, which stands for Volatility, Uncertainty, Complexity, Ambiguity, and, fuck me, if that's not the perfect way to describe a shopping centre visit with two toddlers both struck by sudden-onset diarrhoea, I don't know what is. Whatever work crisis wanted to come at me, I'd flown long haul solo with a teething baby, so I was pretty sure I could handle it.

There are other ways being a mother prepares you well for being a boss. For example, I don't tend to sweat the small stuff. I have boys and if I came running every time someone hollered, I'd do a lot more running than I like to (which is none, ever). My rule is: if it's not bleeding, broken or on fire, it's no big deal. That holds up well in an office full of young women too.

Being a mother when I got my first big job made me determined to not be judged for being a mum, or to make it my whole identity. It has driven me to push myself and my team creatively

because I'm old and resentful of it so I have something to prove. But I've also been well aware that when you become a parent, the first things to go are your love of fresh music, knowledge of cool restaurants and grasp of new vernacular, so rather than being that crotchety gen Xer walking around bitching about millennials and gen Zers, I've always liked to surround myself with people who are cleverer, younger and cooler than I am, who can fill in the cultural gaps for me while I go home at the end of a long working day, make myself a nice cuppa and rewatch *Buffy the Vampire Slayer*. On DVD.

Many of the younger/cleverer/cooler types I surrounded myself with in that first boss gig are still with me, over a decade on. Some left and then came back—nothing pleases my ego so much as a boomerang. Some came later but would be around for the next ten years. Part of this is because I have attachment issues and never want to let anyone go, ever. But it's also because my team is my second family. I've watched them grow up and turn into fully fledged amazing women, writers, designers and stylists. They stuck with me through more babies, working to the dulcet under-the-desk sounds of my breast pump and opening the work fridge to get their yoghurt only to be confronted by rows of multicoloured breastmilk instead. They saw me through a traumatic break-up with the father of my first two children, they followed me to new jobs and businesses, trusting me with their careers even at times when the move might have seemed questionable. I'm never prouder than when seeing the work done by the women who worked for me very early in their careers who went on to do incredible things. It's a better legacy than launching

Elle or winning Editor of the Year and much, much better than *Park Street*, the awful reality TV show ACP forced us to make while I was editor of *Shop* and that we can never, ever unmake.

Once I was in the chair, editing *Shop* was a dream. It was 2008, right in the midst of the GFC, but for us it was like the financial crisis had never happened. The book was always chock-full of ads—more of them than I would have liked were for tampons but I happily took the money. Our sales figures outdid themselves month after month. We had lots of subscribers who dutifully purchased everything we told them to and who resub-scribed each year without needing much bribery or cajoling. We won awards often enough to be quite blasé about it (including the coveted Magazine of the Year).

The best part was that we held a sweet position within the company—consistent enough to be treated with respect and not be in constant fear for our jobs (it was already pretty dog eat dog in there and many of our colleagues didn't have the same privilege) but not important or prestigious enough to be interfered with. This meant that we could get away with all kinds of crazy ideas with various levels of success, from a 3D issue to a crowd-sourced one—and no-one ever bothered to question or stop us. We did issues where everything was under $100, ones where everything was Australian and ones where everything was available online, which in 2011 was actually not an easy task. For that, I received threatening letters and phone calls from various retail bodies who were horrified that I could dream of promoting the dangers of shopping via the internet to the delicate women of Australia, one in particular calling to tell me completely without irony that if I

let the issue go to print, I'd never work in this town again. I bet she felt pretty embarrassed by, say, 2012, when she surely had to realise that the tsunami of e-comm could not be held back by any strategy, bullying or otherwise.

I can't say I was always such a great boss. I'm sure if you ask anyone who has worked for me, they'd only be too willing to recount a story or two of my eccentricities with deeply rolling eyes. I like to think of myself as a closeted graphic designer and have a tendency to sit behind my art directors and design 'with' them, particularly when it comes to covers. Usually this doesn't bother them (or they soon get used to it) but one time a relatively new designer grabbed her handbag and swept herself out from between me and the computer, shrieking 'I can't work like this anymore!', never to be seen again. I reckon she'd probably have some things to say. Also, for a while, every day I'd smuggle my dog into Park Street, which had a strict 'no animals' rule, and have my assistant sneak her out past the security guards in a giant silver Marc Jacobs tote for poops in Hyde Park. I'm not sure if that's better or worse than making my staff talk over the top of my pee, but I know it's up there.

BE CAREFUL WHAT YOU WISH FOR

WHEN I WAS a sixteen-year-old girl, I did the most sixteen-year-old girl thing possible and made a wish book, which was an early incarnation of vision boarding way before *The Secret* was a thing. I still have it in a box somewhere, covered lovingly in pale pink Japanese washi paper and stuffed fat with various pictures and talismans. If I were to make a wish book now, it would be filled with pictures of Celine coats, cars that never need you to stop to fill them up with petrol when you're running late and mothers with naturally perky boobs reading novels on the sofa while their children sit at a table doing craft in absolute silence. But the me of now and the me of sixteen clearly have very different dreams.

On the opening page, there's a long list of all the attributes that I considered vital in a future life partner. Things like: green eyes, surfer, in a band, grew up in the country, must be a fan of Tim Winton. My first partner, the father of my two eldest boys, ticked off pretty much everything on the list, and for this reason I assumed he must be The One, erroneously never realising until

many years and two children later that I had forgotten to specify things like commitment-readiness, shared goals and being in love with me back. They just didn't seem as obviously necessary to a solid lifelong partnership to me back then as, say, being able to play the guitar and a mutual adoration of *Cloud Street*.

The rest of the book is primarily made up of 1990s fragrance ads. There are many, many ads for the Ralph Lauren perfume Romance, every one featuring a ridiculously attractive couple embracing tenderly while standing on a swing in the middle of a field, embracing tenderly while slow-dancing in the middle of a field, embracing tenderly while riding on horseback side by side in the middle of a field. (I didn't underestimate how difficult this feat would be in real life, but that was just evidence, I thought, of the miraculous power of the Ralph Lauren Romance brand of love.)

The ads gave me high expectations for my romantic life and set me up for a lot of disappointment in relationships. Truly, Calvin Klein Eternity is the root cause of so many of my issues. But the ads that started this whole obsession (see what I did there?) were those for Estée Lauder Beautiful, a perfume marketed at brides. There were many incarnations of the Beautiful bride—modest virginal bride, puffy sleeve eighties bride, chic city bride—and through my formative years I'd imagined myself as every single one them.

~

When you don't get married until your mid-thirties and you've based all your romantic aspirations on perfume ads, you've had

lots of time to work out what you want from a wedding. Before I was ever even close to engaged, I knew exactly how I wanted the day to be, down to the last petal. I just needed to fill in the groom. After I broke up with my green-eyed, surfing Tim Winton reader, I looked everywhere for a replacement. I dated what felt like every man alive—the ones who started out great but quickly lost momentum, the ones who started out great but turned out to be secretly married, the ones who started out great but only because I'd had too many cosmos when we first met. At some point, I started to panic. A deep, angsty panic. I panicked that I was on the verge of getting old alone. I panicked that no-one would ever love me with two children in tow. I panicked about the fact that I'd already had one enormous heartbreak in my life and I didn't think I could handle another. And so when I met a lovely man, who was kind and fun and an excellent role model for my boys, I did what seemed to be the sensible thing: I pushed aside any niggling doubts about our chemistry and compatibility and I married him. I didn't give either of us a lot of time to work out if we were particularly suited to each other. Because of the skills of Estée Lauder's creative agency, I could whip the whole thing together in just four months.

~

There were other things in the wish book, alongside all those perfume ads: a company envelope and a 'with compliments' slip from ACP Magazines, where I eventually spent fifteen years of my life, and the cover of the issue of *Elle* which was published when I'd done my very first work experience there. By the time

I was editor of *Shop*, that version of *Elle* magazine had been closed for nearly a decade. But in the years following, the British version had gone on to become the most beloved, highest selling fashion magazine in the world, and rumours were constantly circulating that the brand might be looking to make inroads into Australia again. This was my perennial pipe dream, the magazine I'd dreamt of editing since I was fourteen, clomping around the office nervously in my Docs.

And then it happened. Hearst Corporation in New York announced that they had acquired the rights to *Elle* from its French parent company Lagardère in a number of territories around the world. I felt hopeful that with their existing ACP relationship—they were partners in both *Cosmopolitan* and *Harper's Bazaar*—an Australian relaunch might be on the cards. In the meantime, I was determined to leave nothing to chance. As soon as the Hearst announcement was made, I started work on my pitch—a thirty-page document outlining my ideas for a magazine that the company, as far as I knew, had no definite intention of bringing to our shores. As it turned out, I was right to be so thirsty because just a couple of months later an announcement was made that *Elle* would be relaunched in Australia the following year.

Australians were once famously some of the most avid magazine consumers in the world, which is why we were among the few countries with a population as small as ours to carry such heaving shelves full of titles—including, in the fashion category at that time, local editions of *Marie Claire*, *InStyle*, *Harper's Bazaar*, *Cosmopolitan* and *Vogue*, as well as homegrown titles like *Frankie* and *Russh*. Many people thought it was madness to launch yet

another women's magazine into such a saturated media landscape, but I believed there was a gap in the market for a luxury fashion magazine that was a bit more real and in touch than the ones we were used to, for the kind of woman who loved clothes but didn't let that love define her. I wanted to make a magazine where the focus was not the designers who made the clothes but the women who wore them. I wanted a magazine that reflected how *I* dressed, with a little bit of Balenciaga mixed with a little bit of Zara, and I wanted a magazine that spoke to all the things the smart, successful women I knew cared about—books and music and social trends and politics, not *instead of* but *as well as* shoes and handbags. I wanted to make a magazine that felt like being at a really great dinner party, filled with interesting people—who also just happened to be devastatingly chic. And I imagined a fashion magazine that featured that most stylish and seemingly hard to find accessory of all: a sense of humour.

I was under no false pretences. *Elle* was a massive launch for the company and I knew that management was hoping for a big international name to announce as the editor. I was aware that an internal promotion wasn't quite the sexy announcement they'd been hoping for. But, in my head, I was the only person for the job. Rumours would circulate about other potential editors and I'd feel physically sick and wish bad things upon perfectly nice people. Time passed without much happening except for me getting on important people's nerves. I made another enormous pitch document, this time with thirty-one pages, in case thirty hadn't adequately done the job. I continued to hear crickets.

While all this was happening, I got it into my head that I wanted to have another baby. I was terrified of a pregnancy getting in the way of the job I knew was supposed to be mine but the process—if it was happening at all, which I didn't know because I'd become so annoying that no-one would tell me—was taking so long I figured I had to chance it. At the rate the company moved in these matters, I knew I could very well be menopausal before a decision was made one way or another. I decided to take the leap and work it out—if *it* ever happened—later. Besides, ACP had a solid history of pregnant women making good editors: Ita Buttrose became pregnant just months after launching *Cleo*—much to Kerry's chagrin who apparently complained that she must not have read the story on contraception in her own magazine—and paved the way for working mothers in Australia. If Ita could do it with a magazine named after a long-dead Egyptian queen, I could do it with a masthead as chic and modern as *Elle*.

So I fell pregnant, hoping that a decision would be made quickly so that I could launch the magazine before the baby came. And then as the pregnancy progressed, I hoped that the decision would drag out so that I'd be able to hold off starting on the magazine until after I'd taken some maternity leave. In the end, it was a week before the baby's actual due date—the worst of all the possible timings—that they finally called and asked me to prepare a final presentation for the teams at Hearst in New York and Lagardère in Paris. It's lucky that all my children come late. Scout conveniently held off until I was done with my *third* pitch document—I'm not sure if anyone ever even read the first two—ten days after his due date. And still nothing happened.

And then the phone finally rang. It was mid-summer, stinking hot and I answered it sitting on my sofa in nothing but a pair of maternity knickers because I was three weeks out from having given birth and I didn't have anything weather-appropriate that fit me yet. I had mastitis and I was holding cabbage leaves up to my naked, burning boobs. The heat and the cabbage were not a great combination, aromatically speaking. But the caller had exciting news: the *Elle* teams from New York and Paris were flying into Sydney to meet with both potential advertisers and the ed-in-chief candidates. I was being summoned into the office to give my best Power Editor performance for them in just a few days' time. I hung up the phone and stared down at myself— my swollen breasts, the granny pants, the general aura of having lost any sense of self-respect—horrified but ready. It might not have looked like my moment, but I knew it was.

I cleaned myself up, bought a dress that fit and put a brush to my hair. The interviews went well. I got on with the Americans *and* the French like a house on fire. I felt like finally people other than me understood that this was the job I was born for. And afterwards . . . still nothing.

The enforced showers had renergised me though, and two weeks later, I decided to take the situation in hand. New York Fashion Week was coming up. I'd been there every February for years, always with my friend Bron, the editor of *Cosmo*, where in between the shows we'd walk through the snow in Central Park and eat in all the restaurants we'd read about on Grub Street. Bron and I spent every Valentine's Day for the better part of

a decade drinking bellinis at Pastis after a long day of fashion shows. It was a very romantic time in both our lives.

That year, Bron prepared to go to New York without me while I sat at home despondently with a new baby, lamenting the ratio of dream job offers to maternity pads in my life. Her bosses at Hearst happened to be the same people who were the key decision-makers when it came to *Elle*. I knew that like any good girlfriend, she'd sing my praises while she was there, but the window of opportunity was barely open at this stage and I wished I could do the talking for myself. One day, the baby and I had a good long chat about it and and we decided between us that having waited this long and tried this hard, I may as well go all-in. I packed a hand pump, left the baby and the other boys in the capable hands of my husband and flew myself to New York for two days, tagging along with Bron to the Hearst offices and her work dinners like that annoying fly buzzing around your head you can't seem to swat away. I was going to make them love me. Or if not, I was going to eat my weight in Red Hook Lobster Rolls.

Thank god for that wretched pump. Scout was only six weeks old. I'd used my electric pump like mad in the lead-up so that he'd have enough frozen breastmilk to cover the days I'd be away and this meant that by the time I actually got on the plane, my boobs thought they were feeding octuplets. I had to pump constantly if I wanted any relief or at any time when I required my arms to hang straight by my sides. I pumped in the toilets at Hearst, I pumped in the change rooms at Saks while Bron demanded a deranged stream of different sizes from the salesgirls in an

attempt to buy me more private time in the cubicle, I pumped over fries at The Spotted Pig and cocktails at PDT, while waiting for my foie gras- and brioche-stuffed chicken at The NoMad, and with one hand while lying on Bron's hotel bed eating Magnolia Bakery Banana Pudding with the other. (Really, there's no city on Earth better to be in when you're eating for octuplets.) Then we'd surreptitiously pour that liquid gold down the loo or the gutter on Broadway or Sixth Avenue or wherever we happened to be and I'd get straight back to convincing Hearst why I was the only woman for the job.

And it worked.

I finally started in the role that I'd been dreaming of for more than twenty years when the baby was three months old—straight into a relentless cycle of hostile press interviews, budget negotiations, content plans that needed to be approved across three continents and an intense nationwide advertiser roadshow where I soon learned that my let-down reflex was triggered by boardroom nerves and if I didn't wear two layers of black and multiple breast pads, a milky explosion was guaranteed to happen just as I got to the climax of my presentation.

Dreams really do come true.

HOW TO BE A FASHIONABLE FEMINIST

'THE MOST COURAGEOUS act is still to think for yourself. Aloud,' once said Coco Chanel. You can only imagine she'd be feeling pretty proud of womankind over the past few years, all of us thinking more loudly than ever before. Just as in Coco's time, when she revolutionised fashion to liberate women from the literal physical constraints of the corsets and restrictive clothing that had been before, a generation that was just a decade ago relatively apathetic to the cause of feminism has been permanently awakened to what we need to do in order to effect real change for our generation and future ones. It's part of the reason why, more than a hundred years after opening her first shop, Coco and the legend surrounding her still resonates so strongly with women today. It's about more than just a deep affection for the Boy bag. We're drawn to Coco's rogue spirit, her rebellious attitude and her instinct for change. We don't just want to dress like her—although after all these decades, we'd still wear any one of the outfits she was ever photographed in—we want to *be*

her, with a liberal dose of her *je ne sais quoi* (and her wardrobe of LBDs, *s'il vous plaît*). Growing up, there wasn't anything I wanted more than to visit Coco's Paris. Once grown, I am delighted to discover that landing in the City of Lights never gets boring, even when you're dragging your Rimowa there for work for the fifth time in a year. The other cities on the Fashion Month calendar (referred to only as 'the shows', which makes it sound deceptively fun, like Broadway with even better costumes) are exciting too, of course. London is cool and gritty, New York is bustling and all business, Milan has a steady pace with big shows and lots of ridiculously elegant moments, but it's Paris Fashion Week that is the real circus.

Going to Fashion Week in Paris is theoretically the most glamorous thing in the world. And I think it actually is for some people—Olivia Palermo, Sienna Miller, people with every possible resource who are actually just there to see and be seen, looking achingly fashionable while doing it. But the experience for the vast majority of the rest of the attendees is completely different. For us, it is a slog—albeit a very chic, inspiring slog, but a slog nonetheless.

Imagine, if you will, a giant school camp, except the campers are everyone you work with, have ever worked with and might ever work with, along with some Kardashians. Instead of a camping ground, the campers descend on an entire city. You know when you go to a work conference and the Marriott becomes like a little microcosm of your work universe where you bump into people you know everywhere—in the gym, at the breakfast buffet, awkwardly in the halls when you're sneaking out of Josh from

Accounts Payable's room at 4 am? Fashion Week is exactly like that, just replace the words 'the Marriott' with 'all of Paris'. (And Josh, instead of being from Accounts, is more likely to be a photographer, cinematographer, male model or . . . nope, that's it.) It's such a city takeover that the taxi drivers all have the show schedule printed out and stuck to their sunshades and will happily tell you their thoughts on the Acne collection from that morning if you give them even a hint of an opening.

Instead of cabins, it's hotel suites, with the most popular kids (say, those with a half a million-plus followers on Instagram) staying at the Plaza Athénée, the Ritz, Le Meurice, Le Bristol, the Peninsula or the super secretive Hôtel de Pourtalès where Kim Kardashian was famously robbed at gunpoint, and everyone else staying in 'boutique' hotels with genuine *Fawlty Towers* vibes, where the only place to keep your suitcase is on top of your toilet when you're not using it.

At either end of the fashion food chain, this is no mellow city break. There's a fashion show about every two hours across the week, including Saturday and Sunday. Some are small and intimate, while others—Dior, Chanel, Saint Laurent—are enormous and bring the city to a standstill, taking over actual monuments with crowds of hardcore fashion fans and gape-mouthed tourists all pushed up against barricades waiting for a glimpse of Rihanna or Anna Wintour like teenage fans at a One Direction concert, and just as likely to see Harry Styles.

In between the shows or when you're skipping a show or if—*quelle horreur*—you're not invited to a show, you are still busy, busy, busy—visiting showrooms, meeting designers, PR contacts,

agents and photographers, wooing advertisers. Every minute of every day is absorbed by Important Fashion Business, starting from your very first morning meeting until you fall into bed after the very last event, usually a party after dinner (which might not even start until 11 pm, because this is Europe). Do this for a week and you'll see why fashion people tend to be thin. There's no time to eat. To be at Fashion Week is to be doing enforced intermittent fasting, with dinner your only meal of the day. Actually, sometimes there is a moment at some point in the late afternoon for a *vin rouge* and some *frites* at Hôtel Costes, unless you use that time to get changed into a second outfit for the day. If I have one rule for life it's this: *always choose the frites*.

The schedule takes you all over the city. A car with a driver is very necessary, and rarely something I ever managed to have signed off by a finance department, who always considered Fashion Month a long, fancy junket to be resented and made as difficult as possible. French taxis are notoriously hard to find, particularly after a big show in an outer arrondissement with crowds of people all needing to get to the next show pronto. Sometimes a girl—usually me—could be brought to tears by the frustration of being stranded in heels with no option of getting to the next show in time aside from racing across cobblestone streets on agonised foot. Thank the sweet lord for the relatively recent invention of Uber, which transformed the Fashion Week experience into an altogether less painful one. Then again, the challenges of trying to explain in broken French to an Uber driver which person in *noir* in a huge sea of other people in *noir* you are is its own sweet agony.

The true evolution in the Fashion Week experience was the rise of the flat shoe, possibly the only time in existence when a fashion item has been described by an editor as 'life-changing' and it is actually true. Our salvation crept up on us. First, certain brands of ballet slipper took on cult status—Chanel, Ferragamo, Lanvin—but unless you were Audrey Hepburn they were mostly just used to get from A to B then stashed in a bag big enough to hide them in when you arrived at your destination and needed to put on your 'real' shoes. Then Isabel Marant showed us how much we enjoyed the streetwear appeal of a hi-top while still getting the flattering leg lift of a concealed heel, an ingenious gateway drug to sneakers, although we didn't know it at the time. Around the same time, It-girls such as Poppy Delevingne and Alexa Chung started demonstrating how cute a brogue could be, although you seemed to need to actually have Alexa or Poppy's legs to pull them off. Then Chloé ankle boots took over our weekends. At some point, Birkenstocks had a hipster revival and then suddenly every brand from Givenchy to Balenciaga released their own version of an orthopaedic-looking slide: the chunky sandal officially went mainstream. But not all the flat shoes popping up around us were of the ugly but cool variety: Valentino did impressive things with their elegant point-toed Rockstud flat and Gucci reinvented the loafer, which culminated in the kangaroo fur-lined versions that led to waitlists and queues the world over.

With magic timing, all this aligned perfectly with the fashion world's complete surrender to athleisurewear, when the humble sneaker turned into the status shoe du jour, thanks to Phoebe Philo and her Stan Smiths.

All this marked a seismic shift in our attitudes to footwear. Even that over-achieving blonde Barbie—who had somehow managed numerous successful careers, including that of a paratrooper, cowgirl and cat burglar, all in heels—was finally granted a flat-shoe-wearing foot at the ripe age of fifty-six, which is more than long enough for anyone to be on tiptoes, even if her injection molded plastic feet were made to be that way. Meanwhile, at the shows, the proliferation of flat shoes on front rowers increased, season after season, until it surpassed its trend/novelty status to become the new normal. The fashion world had tasted comfort and freedom for the first time since, well, ever, and we liked it. At least between the hours of 6 am to 6 pm anyway.

The joys we're now discovering in trainers and loafers and chunky sandals goes well beyond just sole comfort—it's also about a longer stride, a quickened pace, an increased stamina. Who can forget the crippling arches and unmistakable misery of standing as still as possible at a work cocktail party, eleven hours into your day in four-inch heels, wondering how you'd even make it to the cab rank when sweet home time eventually did arrive? I love a great shoe as much as the next girl, but now I feel that they're best considered decorative art pieces to gaze at lovingly in your open-shelf wardrobe or for shooting within a highly styled Instagram flat-lay. We're not meant to actually *wear* them. The shoe revolution has brought with it freedom and strength, and while the appeal of a fun, strappy party sandal is irrefutable, it cannot even come close to that. Carrie Bradshaw lived in a different world.

Like all the most important fashion trends, this one is perfectly aligned to the times we're living in. As feminism has become a compelling force in our culture, fashion has done its best to stay abreast. It hasn't always got it right (the industry's snail-like pace in embracing curvy fashion despite ever-increasing demand is a perfect example) but when it comes to our wardrobes, there's a lot about the past few years that has been deeply empowering for women whether we know it or not—and I'm not just talking about politically charged slogan tees. From activewear for everyday to soft-cup bras, the way we dress today has all been designed to allow us to move, to keep up and to look more like ourselves.

The cross-body bag, for example, is a trend so subtle that you could almost not recognise it as a trend at all until you remember back to the noughts and how we all walked around encumbered by weighty Balenciaga Lariat top-handle totes (or their numerous imitators) in the crooks of our elbows. A colleague of mine used to say, 'the bigger the bag is, the smaller the arse looks' and I considered this as close to diet advice as I would ever get. As a result, I had a permanent red welt on my arm where the strap of my enormous bag hung, and hands that were always on the verge of tissue death due to lack of blood supply, but I put up with it because I thought it made me look petite, like an Olsen. The cross-body, on the other hand, allows us to move about this life with both hands free to make and do things, hold our babies and give someone you love a proper hug without a patent leather barrier between you. Recently, I've even started forgoing any bag at all in favour of just my iPhone and I always feel extra adept and nimble for doing so. Once upon a time, it felt positively

dangerous to be out without two lip balms, a rosewater face spray, every store card I'd ever signed up for, breath mints, a Tide stain remover pen, hand sanitiser and every key to every door I might never want to open. Now I've realised I don't need any of it at all. Who knew? Well, men knew. No wonder we weren't able to rule the world before this: we weren't dressed for it.

All of this is just a continuation of what Coco started all those years ago. If our feet feel less painful these days, the time line can be traced right back to her. Long before the pussy hat, she created the first feminist wardrobe, getting rid of unwieldy brims and corsets in favour of looser clothing that gave women's bodies room to breathe and freedom to move. (Another of my favourite quotes from Coco was about the millinery of the time: 'How can a brain function under those things?'—which is exactly how I felt years later about those influencer favourite felt numbers.) She ran her own business and was, by and large, financially independent, in that she never relied on a husband, although she wasn't against using her feminine wiles to help her along where necessary.

~

On one of my trips to Paris, I was invited to Coco's apartment above the store at 31 Rue Cambon, which has been impeccably maintained just as it was when she held it. (She didn't officially 'live' there—she slept across the road at the Ritz. Why? Because she was Coco-fucking-Chanel.) To me, the visit felt like more than just a trip to a particularly intimate museum—it was the closest I'd ever come to a spiritual pilgrimage. Not just as a fashion aficionado surrounded by beautiful things and at the source of

so much iconography of a brand that we all know so well but because of the place that Coco holds in women's history. I sat in her apartment, on the very same deep suede sofa where Pablo Picasso and Salvador Dalí would have sat next to her and talked art and politics and passions, and I thanked her, from my heart to the soles of my pain-free, flat-shodden feet.

EXCESS BAGGAGE

BEING THE EDITOR of a prestigious fashion magazine is both much more magic than you can ever imagine and much more mundane. Because you're running a business, there are spreadsheets to fill out and KPIs to meet, management meetings to try not to sleep through and vaguely threatening team emails to send about exciting issues such as courier expenditure. As much as an editor might think it's her right—nay, her *duty*—to swan around the office yelling 'Think pink!' at hapless assistants and innocent mail boys, she is nonetheless required to perform all the standard pen-pushing duties that come with any upper-middle management job. I won't bore you with the details of it here. What makes all that bearable, though, are those magic bits. And there are many.

One time for a Resort show, I flew to London with Dior, to stay at the Dorchester. They'd transformed an iconic Soho pub into the Lady Dior Inn, where everything from the signage hanging over the door to the beer mats and the coasters had been rebranded Lady Dior, and where I sang karaoke until late

into the night with the editors of other top fashion magazines around the world. (Pro tip: at any international fashion event, the Australians and Brazilians are always the last to leave the dance floor. We're committed like that.)

The next day we caught a luxury train to Blenheim Palace. The train had been magically transformed into an haute couture take on the Hogwarts Express—the 'Dior Express'—and was just as movie-worthy, maybe more so because rather than the Weasley brothers the train staff were all devastatingly handsome male models wearing top to toe Dior Homme with jaunty little Dior conductor hats that I will later deeply regret not having the chutzpah to nick. Inside the palace, we watched the runway show in rooms once slept in by real kings and queens, and then partied in a ballroom the size of a basketball stadium, so full of towering cakes and delicate pastries that Marie Antoinette would have felt miffed. No-one ate anything, of course, because as the saying goes, 'You'll never be cold in couture because you're never waiting for a bus, but lord knows you can still get fat.' It looked incredible, though, and in fashion that is always the point. Luckily, I was carrying a clutch large enough to hold no less than four raspberry macarons, which I snuck out and devoured happily in the back of the chauffeur-driven Bentley on my way back to the hotel.

I was once flown to Marrakech, the mecca for all Talitha Getty-wannabes like me, to celebrate the fiftieth anniversary of a Van Cleef & Arpels necklace. Yes, birthday parties for necklaces are a thing that happens in the world of high fashion. We stayed at La Mamounia, where Poppy Delevingne got married, and had dinner in an abandoned sixteenth-century palace, the grounds

and moat of which were lit by a million white candles in a scene that was as close as I think I will ever get to heaven on Earth.

I've been to New York City with Tiffany & Co. for the launch of their famed Blue Book collection, which is a good thing to do if you ever want to feel in equal parts privileged to be part of such a rarefied world and deeply bitter about your lack of mattresses stuffed with $500 bills back home. Tiffany's best customers from across the globe are flown in for the event each year. On arrival in their hotel rooms, they find a book—essentially a jewellery catalogue but *just* a little bit fancier than your average Angus & Coote version—featuring a limited collection of incredible one-off rings, bracelets and necklaces available to purchase the next day, in a predetermined order. I get anxiety at a Bassike sample sale, so I can only imagine the stress involved if you have your heart set on a particular six-figure 23 karat tanzanite and diamond ring and have to wait all day for your turn to find out if an MIP (More Important Person) ahead of you on the list got to it first so the only thing left available to you is the six-figure sea anenome-shaped sapphire brooch. But if there's any buyer's remorse or jewel-based rivalry between any of the guests they put it aside that night to celebrate the world's most glamorous shopping weekender at a gala event, where security guards hover around the edge of the dance floor protecting the blinding baubles adorning their lucky new owners' fingers, necks and wrists as they cut a rug alongside Reese Witherspoon and Zoë Kravitz. It's quite the humdinger.

I once witnessed Chanel transform the Grand Palais in Paris into an airport complete with check-in desks and baggage carou-sels, another time into a magical woodland with actual full-sized

trees and a carpet of real autumn leaves, and another into a faux building-lined avenue featuring a swarm of supermodel protesters. I was there for the famed shopping centre show where the space, as big as an airport hangar, became the Chanel Supermarché. Hundreds of actual grocery products lined the shelves, cleverly redesigned on-brand, with a breakfast cereal offering called 'Coco Flakes' and deli meat labelled 'Jambon Cambon' after the street where Gabrielle's first shop and apartment still stands. I hadn't realised I could ever feel so longingly for tea bags ('Little Black Tea'). As the show ended, Cara Delevingne pushed Rihanna around in an oversized trolley holding a huge bottle of 'Tweed' Riesling as though they were stocking up at the local Dan Murphy's on the first day of schoolies, and a man's voice came over the loudspeaker, saying in both English and French, 'Thank you for coming to Le Grand Supermarché de Chanel. Please exit through the check-outs and don't forget to take your complimentary bo—' He apparently finished with the word 'bonbons' but no-one heard. At 'complimentary', hundreds of frenzied front rowers leapt from their seats and descended on the aisles, shoving anything not nailed down into limited edition Boy bags and vintage 2.55s. Of course, we Australians had too much of our natural antipodean inferiority complex to partake in this manic supermarché sweep, but from our spot in front of the homewares department (think Chanel-does-Bunnings—if they'd served sausage sambos there I would have been in actual heaven), I witnessed some of the world's most famously elegant people literally clamber over each other in a mad scramble to steal doormats emblazoned with the Coco Mademoiselle logo. It was proof that, no matter what her social

status, there's not a lot a woman wouldn't be prepared to do in the name of free Chanel, even when it's just the pretend packaging of an empty box of double-C-branded beef bouillon stock cubes.

Another time, Karl and his team took over the Ritz Paris for a Métiers d'Art show (the annual collection designed to celebrate the makers and artisans that contribute to Chanel collections) and afterwards we sang more international fashion industry karaoke— it's a thing—in the tiny Ritz Bar. At one point, the song 'Happy' came on and I realised the person who'd programmed it was Pharrell, there in the flesh doing karaoke to his own tune. I immediately cancelled my request for Dolly's '9 to 5', and then facetimed my kids to tell them I was in the room with the guy who sings the Minions song. That's when I knew I was officially old.

I've sipped cocktails in Christian Dior's family home, eaten sea urchins with Bella Hadid in Tokyo and laid by the pool at Hôtel du Cap-Eden-Roc next to Natalie Portman. I was there when U2 played a surprise private performance at the Apple Music launch in Cupertino, California, when the room full of tech nerds clapped politely from their seats after the performance but then minutes later jumped to their feet and screamed with excitement as the new iPhone was announced. Even a relatively normal day on the fashion circuit might have involved sitting front row at the Hermès show (a thoughtful blanket on your seat to keep your lap warm in the early spring outdoor setting), being low-key delighted to find that Miu Miu has delivered their latest bag to your hotel room while you were out, feeling so overwhelmed by emotion that you're brought to actual tears by the extreme beauty of a Valentino collection, then being surprised

by a private Will Smith performance over supper to celebrate a Louis Vuitton store opening. (There's nothing European fashion loves more than ironic pop culture nostalgia and it's hard to not get swept up in their enthusiasm.)

These moments of such extreme privilege and spectacle and money-can't-buy experiences (that actually money *can* buy, but just not the sort of money most of us non-oligarchs will ever see in our lifetimes) made the more real, less glamorous parts of the job worth it. And even at its most mundane, there are worse ways to make a living than being surrounded by beautiful things in a job where spending half an hour convincing someone to buy the new season Loewe bag is considered a successful meeting.

~

That world isn't quite the same anymore. The magazine teams (most of them) have vanished into thin air and Covid-19 has put a final end to the vicious cycle of seasons and collections and relentless chasing of newness that creatively exhausted designers and travel-weary editors and buyers have all been trapped in for years. It's been a circuit-breaker that has enabled an industry known for constant *more* to finally be able to choose *less*. The pandemic has given the industry the chance to take a moment to try to come up with solutions to the problems that have been plaguing it ever since the global financial crisis—a calendar that was a huge mess, with shows and the attention given to them happening months before pieces were available to buy, deliveries that weren't relevant to the seasons, with coats going on sale in summer and bikinis in winter, and a hamster wheel of promotions and sales that no-one

could afford to jump off. A year without much newness (aside from a whole lot of tracksuit pants and hoodies) has forced everyone to slow down, catch up and think about how things could work better. This, mixed with a customer who cares more and more that her wardrobe is sustainable and ethically made, and the new necessary mood of economic austerity—where the kind of decadence and extravagance we'd grown used to suddenly feels decidedly *out* of fashion—has changed the face of the fashion industry, at least for the time being.

Will we miss the spectacle of it, of all that relentless newness? Maybe a little. But this is not the end of fashion. Because what we suddenly find ourselves wanting now has turned out to be so much better. Clothing that has nothing to do with seasonal trends and everything to do with how it makes us feel when we wear it. Beautiful, timeless pieces that bring us so much joy we want to put them on over and over again, for years to come. Stripped of the extravagance, the circus and the excess, we've finally discovered the real magic of fashion.

COVER SHOOTS AND OTHER CATASTROPHES

THERE'S NOTHING SO magic in the world of magazine publishing as the cover. Even though magazines have lost their place at the top of the media pecking order, covers are still prime real estate— lusted over, aimed for, analysed, liked, posted and reported on. Pretty much everything except purchased. Even as influencers have grown in power, with their follower counts in many cases far greater than the audiences any magazine can claim, many of them still consider a cover the ultimate prize. Turns out that even people with a thriving Instagram Live presence like to be able to give their grans something tangible to show off to the ladies at bingo.

Pulling together a cover should be simple. You have a cover star in mind, you speak to her people, you book a crew and a studio or location, and you take some pictures. But it's not nearly as easy as all that. First, you have to think of someone you'd like to run, which is sometimes difficult in itself. They have to be a person who is interesting to your readers, 'on brand' for your

masthead and having a bit of a moment. They can't have been on your cover in the past year or any of your competitors' covers for the past six months, and they have to be famous and liked enough to hopefully sell their socks off. As my time as an editor went on, these mythical unicorns were getting harder and harder to find. I missed the days in the late noughts when we could just chuck Mischa Barton on the cover and know everything would be okay. No-one didn't love Mischa. I don't know where it all went wrong, for her or us.

Hovering over you like an ominous cheap perfume as you make these decisions is the very real fear of failure—and being fired. An editor's career can be made or broken on the covers she runs, so there isn't a lot of room for error. It might be easier if we had more Australian celebrities with the pulling power to sell mags, but there are just not enough Nicoles, Naomis, Cates and Margots to go around, so we most often need to look above our station to international stars for the plum spot. Unfortunately, this means needing to convince a generally scary Hollywood publicist of the value of letting their client spend a day shooting for a little Australian magazine with our little Australian numbers, when that day could be allocated to a magazine in, say, China, and reach about a billion more people. And even if they like you, they still have to decide whether your proposed cover date works for when they have a project to promote, go for your shoot concept, approve the photographer and hair and make-up teams, and, once convinced, find a date said celebrity can be available to shoot between filming or touring or hanging out in Montauk with their new secret boyfriend. Once all that's worked out . . . then

you have to then find a way to pay for the shoot (because your measly mag budget in this day and age will never be enough), pray the celebrity doesn't cancel or change the dates after you buy the crew five non-refundable discounted economy fares to LA on a sponsor's dime, choose a location unseen from the other side of the world, fill a styling rack with clothes they might refuse to wear, find a caterer who doesn't cook with meat, dairy, gluten, sugar or actual food and hope that it doesn't rain on the day because the budget doesn't allow for a backup weather hold.

And if by some miracle of god you actually manage to take some pictures: well, don't for a minute assume your work is done, you silly fool. After the shoot, you need to find an angle for an article worthy of a cover profile when your chosen one doesn't want to talk about anything at all, especially not that new boyfriend which is all any of your readers really care about, and select an image that has the perfect amount of eye contact, energy and body shape in an outfit by an advertiser important enough to have been promised a cover. You have to also cross your fingers that your cover talent doesn't make any moves in the three months between shooting and publication that will make your long-lead story yesterday's news in an instant. She can't shave her head when your cover features waist-length locks (this has actually happened to me), get married to or break up with the boyfriend (happened to me), announce a pregnancy (yup) or have been involved in any kind of scandal between when you go to print and when you land on the newsstand (*so many* have happened to me).

~

Literally as I'm writing this chapter, my phone beeps. It's a message telling me that the musician Flume, who we've just shot at great expense in LA to run on the cover of a relatively conservative magazine I'm working on, is all over the news. I click the link I've been sent. The headline reads: 'FLUME EATS ASS AT BURNING MAN'.

You can't make this shit up.

~

Whenever you shoot a cover, everyone wants to know what the talent is like. By and large, because it's a prerequisite of their job to be charming and they know you're going to write a story about them, they're mostly very nice. One of the most impressive examples of professionalism I ever witnessed on a cover shoot was from Australian supermodel Elle Macpherson. She was being photographed by her ex-husband, the legendary French photographer Gilles Bensimon (a situation that really would be tricky enough), who wanted to shoot on a yacht on Sydney Harbour, out past the heads. The sea was rough and one by one each of the *Elle* staff—including me—was struck down with violent seasickness. We vomited so much in the bathroom of the boat that one of the deckhands was sent below deck by the skipper to stop us from blocking the toilet and to insist that we vomit above board, over the side of the yacht, instead. My fashion director, Rachel, normally a sweet, gentle soul, gripped the poor deckhand by the shoulders, stared at him with pure terror in her eyes and said, 'You *cannot* make me vomit in front of Gilles Bensimon!' Alas, he did not give in. For the rest of the day, she, I and the rest of

the team—everyone, in fact, except Gilles—hung over the sides of the boat, loudly hurling, only able to show our approval for shots via a weak thumbs-up.

Elle was also sick. She just took a minute to grip the side of the boat before getting back into position as quickly as she could and showing no signs of the nausea she was experiencing, except for looking a tiny bit green around the gills—something that the retoucher easily dealt with afterwards. It was the least we could do.

This is the sort of behaviour you can expect from most cover stars, especially the really famous international ones, who tend to be unfailingly professional, if a little temperamental. It's the next tier down who always surprise you, like Lea Michele from *Glee*, who—in just one of many on-set 'moments'—kicked a shoe at my fashion director and made her cry. She was . . . unpleasant.

~

I only ever commit to writing a cover profile myself if I think I'm really, really going to like the person, because I'm too honest to write gushingly about someone I don't like and a cover story needs to gush a little bit, otherwise why are you putting them on your cover? ('Availability' apparently not being a good enough answer to that question.) Sometimes I've gotten that wrong. I didn't write Isla Fisher's cover story because I wasn't certain that she'd be forthcoming, and I regretted it because she was excellent company and when she told me she thought her personality didn't come off well in print, I felt sad that I wouldn't be able to help remedy that. I did write Rebel Wilson's thinking we'd walk out best friends, but completely underestimated how Hollywood she was, and I

found it nearly impossible to break though the dark glasses and entourage. Olivia Palermo, back when *The City* was a thing we cared about, was a surprise. Far from being the cold, snobby Manhattan princess I thought I knew from her 'reality' show, she lived in Brooklyn and gave me outlet shopping tips. On the other hand, Chrissy Teigen is everything you want her to be and more. Her rider demanded three different specific types of turkey jerky by brand name and flavour and a completely unspecific request for 'red wine' and 'white wine', which has to be the most wonderfully unpretentious thing I've ever heard.

~

Some months on a magazine it can feel like there isn't going to be a cover at all. Talent drops out, replacements aren't available, potential syndications from overseas aren't approved to run in Australia. The deadline approaches, coming closer and closer, bringing with it a wild panic, sleepless nights, cold sweats and the editor's life flashing before her eyes. But something always comes through to save our skin at the last minute. Except for the one time when it didn't.

The issue was a special one celebrating Australian woman-hood. We shot a beautiful portrait series for inside the book, from a one-month-old baby girl to my creative director's 100-year-old gran, and interviewed women and girls of all different ages and life paths about their hopes and dreams, challenges and achievements. It was one of my favourite issues yet. The question was who to put on the cover of such an issue. They had to be Australian, of course, but not just any actress or model would have done—they

had to somehow represent all of us. I obsessed over it for weeks and came up blank.

Eventually, I pitched an idea to my publisher that I'd been mulling over for a while but had never been brave enough to run: replacing the usual image on the cover with a mirror, making the reader the cover star. A risk, yes, but not really, given that we had no alternative anyway.

The mirror ended up being one of our most talked about covers ever, and no-one ever suspected that it was actually a cunning last-minute save of what was about to be a complete disaster.

That mirror cover was hugely successful in almost every way—advertisers, social media, the press, everyone loved it . . . except, that was, for paying magazine consumers. They didn't buy it. In fact, in my experience, none of the really exciting covers that got a lot of attention were ever the biggest sellers. Not the mirror cover, or the one we shot on an iPhone, which made news around the world for being a global first. Not the one we made of model Gemma Ward with five different head shots sliced into thirds like a kids' flip book allowing readers to mix up Gemma's eyes, lips and hair to make thirty-five different beauty looks, which won Cover of the Year and was endlessly copied in other markets. People loved these covers—and advertisers loved them which meant they were considered successful in a different way—but the huge amounts of publicity they got were never reflected in their sales. In my experience, the covers that sold best were the safe ones, preferably of a blonde your nan recognised from free-to-air TV or literally anyone who shared a bloodline with Kris Jenner.

Not that I ever stopped trying. One time, watching Mick Fanning get attacked by a shark during a surfing contest on the news, I knew it was a moment the world would be talking about for months to come and decided then and there that I had to put him on the cover of *Elle*.

Unfortunately, he wasn't as keen on this idea as I was. Not traditionally a fashion guy, he was sceptical about agreeing to a fashion magazine cover. He was also getting offers from Jimmy Fallon and *60 Minutes* and all kinds of more exciting and important places than us. We went back and forth for ages trying to make it happen and I was just about to give up when I found myself at the local primary school open day along with Mick's manager and Simon Upton, the photographer we wanted to use, whose kids both attended the same school as mine. We came to an agreement right there in the halls.

My vision was of Mick, an Australian superhero, alongside Jess Hart, an Australian supermodel, in the ocean for our summer cover. With Mick and Jess on board, our next step was to find a place in the world where he (constantly travelling the globe in the race for the world title), she (a jetsetting model mostly based in NYC, and back then occasionally on Greek yachts), Simon (in and out of the country on shoots) and myself and my fashion director, Rachel (about to head off on the international fashion week circuit), could all be in the one place at the same time. This process of back and forth and getting nowhere took years off my life, but we eventually homed in on one single possible date and location—just days away and in outer Los Angeles, close to where Mick was competing in a surfing contest.

Naively, we started to think we had it in the bag, but as soon as we'd booked our unrefundable flights, Jess's Australian agent realised her New York agent had accidentally double-booked her on another job in NYC for that entire week. Many swearwords passed my lips as we waited nervously for this to be sorted, which took much longer than my nerves could handle.

At least, we assumed, booking the location would be easy. The one thing LA is full of—along with great sushi, douchey guys and free pour drinks—is amazing locations. Or so we thought. But that single lonely day we could shoot happened to be a Saturday— the Saturday of Labor Day weekend to be precise, a public holiday and the very last weekend of the American summer, the one you're not supposed to wear white after. This meant it was literally impossible to get a permit to shoot on the beach anywhere in the whole of LA. Not giving up so easily, we searched for houses with private beaches, but as it turned out, anyone who had one of those wanted to use it themselves on Labor Day weekend. (Jerks. But also understandable. Let's be friends?)

I was starting to wonder if we should shoot them in the bathtub of my hotel room when we finally found a perfect spot. We boarded a flight and everyone started to breathe normally, even me. There was plane drinking involved. So it should come as no surprise at all that an hour into the fourteen-hour trip, our creative director back at home received a call: the owners of the dream house had gone AWOL and the location had been pulled. With less than a day until the shoot and nowhere to shoot it, she was forced to book the only other even partly suitable location she could find, which of course happened to be a two-hour

drive from where we were booked to stay—with a 5 am call time the next day.

While our hotel was no longer anywhere near our new shoot location, as things turned out it was just a twenty-minute drive from Disneyland, so we did the only sensible thing to do the night before a very important cover shoot following weeks of anxiety: we hotfooted it to Space Mountain. And just like that, the shoot that had until that point felt completely cursed was sprinkled with magic dust (or, actually, magic snow, Elsa-style).

This is just a typical example of the roller-coaster of emotion that goes into the birthing of a cover, not dissimilar to the birthing of a child: both are painful, vomit-inducing experiences with just enough legitimate fear to make you slightly delirious and occasionally soil yourself. But after all the trauma is over and you hold that creation in your hands for the first time, show it off to your friends and family, and post incessantly and annoyingly about it on Instagram, you know that all the pain was worth it—until the next time.

UNDER COVER

I STOOD AND knocked tentatively on my publisher's office door, holding a printout of my latest cover gingerly in my fingertips, bringing it to her like an offering. As a new editor, the process was a nerve-racking one. The cover I held in my sweaty hands this time was Beyoncé, and she looked . . . well, she looked like Beyoncé. She looked perfect.

The publisher held the cover in her hands and looked at it approvingly. 'It's wonderful,' she nodded. I gave a relieved little sigh and turned to leave the room. But just as I got to the door, she glanced back up from her computer screen and piped up, nonchalantly, as though having an afterthought, 'Are you going to make her skin a little lighter?'

I was shook, not really sure if she was joking. I stammered something incomprehensible in response and ran through the halls in a mad panic to get to my art director, who'd been around longer than me and who confirmed for me that this was an actual thing. 'Black cover stars don't sell in Australia,' I was constantly

told by everyone who should know. And neither, I'd be told at other times, do Asians, plus-sized bodies, pregnant people, freckles or redheads.

After a round of retouching—and, yes, skin lightening—I took the cover back for a second round of approvals. She popped it on her wall and stepped back to take look. 'Lovely,' she nodded. But just as I was about to walk out the door, she called again, like it was the first time she'd thought of it, 'Are you going to make her skin a little lighter?' I didn't know whether to laugh or cry.

Not long after that, I was asked to do the same thing to Eva Mendes's skin, at which point my brain promptly exploded. This was back in the early days of retouching, when magazine publishers were drunk on the relatively new power in their hands. Cover stars were not only made smoother, slimmer and whiter but sometimes given Frankenstein-style makeovers, with different shots of a model's head and body being mixed and matched, or sometimes a head being patched onto someone else's body altogether. Thank god the industry eventually learned the error of its ways with a liquifying tool, but some real atrocities occurred before it did.

~

Before diversity became a hot commodity that the magazine publishing industry could no longer ignore, magazine editors were constantly coming under fire for the lack of any on their covers. In our defence, it wasn't for want of trying. There's a belief that editors are the final word when it comes to covers, but often— especially when an editor is new to the role—they need to get

their covers signed off by a publisher or some sort of corporate management team, who are generally as knowledgeable about women as they sound, and always go for the safe option.

And from the advent of celebrity covers in the nineties until not that long ago, it was pretty much impossible to argue for anything different when almost all the covers that sold well featured very famous, very pretty, very skinny blondes. This led to a monotonous cycle of confirmation bias that definitely held magazines back from evolving as they needed to over the years. Thankfully, this sort of primitive decision-making went on much less once the socials were born and magazine sales dwindled to the point where the revenue from copy sales was no longer nearly as important a part of the equation as advertising dollars were. Suddenly, likes mattered more, because advertisers liked likes, and if advertisers liked your likes, they were more likely to give you their money. Which, if you were someone who didn't like to play it so safe, like me, was not such a bad thing.

Not that the perception of needing to fit the cookie-cutter cover mould ever completely went away. I wasn't allowed to run Rebel Wilson on the cover for a long time at *Elle*, because she apparently 'wouldn't sell', which was publisher code for 'Not a size 0'. (Eventually I did get to put her on the cover and she sold just fine.)

~

My favourite ever cover was the one we ran at *Elle* of model Nicole Trunfio breastfeeding her baby, Zion. It wasn't a pre-planned moment, as much as I'd like to claim that I masterminded it

from the beginning. Nicole and Zion were on set being photographed and he got hungry mid-shoot, so Nicole fed him—because when your new baby is hungry, you feed him whether you're standing under a bunch of lights wearing a one-off sample of a new season Burberry Prorsum trench from the runway or otherwise. Our photographer, Georges Antoni, snapped a picture in that moment and when I stumbled upon it in the edit, my heart skipped a beat.

The shot turned out to be the world's very first magazine cover ever of a woman breastfeeding—aside from the *Time* magazine cover which had a full-sized human child standing at his mother's breast, which doesn't count because it didn't so much #normalisebreastfeeding as #makeeveryonefeelickyaboutbreastfeeding. But while it was widely celebrated for being a beautiful depiction of motherhood, I was still criticised for running it only on our subscriber edition, which apparently implied that breastfeeding was something to be ashamed of. Anyone who knew how many times I'd answered the door to the Thai delivery guy without remembering to put my own boobs back in when my children were babies would attest to the fact that I find nothing shameful in that particular activity, but according to my critics, the only way to champion breastfeeding 'properly' would have been to put it on the newsstand cover.

Unfortunately, running the breastfeeding cover as the *only* cover was never going to have happened. In the minds of management, this cover was already considered a risk. Model instead of actress? Risk. Local talent instead of internationally famous superstar? Risk. Not Jennifer Aniston? Definite risk. Boob in

a baby's mouth even though you would have seen more skin if Nicole had been in a bikini? Risk, risk, risk. Just a few complaints to Woolworths or Coles could have been enough to have the magazine pulled from the shelves and kill my sales for the month. It might have required me to have stickers manually placed over the offending boob/baby's head at hideous expense. My job was to run a business, and that business was selling magazines. As such, the only alternative I had to not running Nicole feeding Zion as a subscriber cover was to not run it at all. But the publishing business model was hard to magsplain in a twenty-second soundbite on television. And it was demoralising to have to defend the cover at all for that reason when there I'd been, naively thinking we were using our platform to revive a conversation about something so worthwhile.

~

The criticism that you can't do something good unless you do it *enough* is one that magazine editors cop a lot. Robbie Myers, once my US counterpart on *Elle*, was constantly under fire every time she put anyone who wasn't white or didn't look like a supermodel on the cover. She was slammed if they were wearing too many clothes, or not enough clothes, or if she'd run a head shot, or a full-length one, or if the image was in black and white. Never mind that they were the only American fashion magazine running Gabourey Sidibe and Melissa McCarthy and Mindy Kaling on a cover in the first place and the shots were universally stunning. Similarly, Australian magazines had been running a revolving line-up of same-same pretty starlets and models on their covers

for years, never even attempting to show a different perspective. At *Elle*, we ran groundbreaking racially and size diverse covers well before it was in fashion, but I still had to defend myself and my business choices on breakfast TV. It was enough to make me look at my colleagues at *Gourmet Traveller* and fantasise about a world where the biggest cover drama I'd encounter would be whether to run the chocolate lava cake or the pork belly.

One day my deputy editor and I were sitting in my office throwing ideas around when the topic of Lara Bingle came up. She was still tabloid fodder, but we both found her a guilty pleasure. We decided to put her on the cover, thinking that all that *Daily Mail* traffic couldn't be wrong. Not everyone thought this was as good an idea as we did. Lara would go on to become cover gold, that rare beast who could almost always guarantee sales and had luxury brands flocking to dress her, but that was all a way off—she was yet to earn her fashion chops. Lots of international designer brands wouldn't loan clothes to us for the shoot because they wouldn't approve Lara to wear them. Lots of people within the company questioned our thinking and I had to go into battle multiple times to even get it off the ground.

Just after the shoot, I got a new publisher. I was called to her office for our very first meeting and, again, I found myself knocking tentatively, holding my printed-out offering. The new publisher greeted me brusquely, flicking her eyes straight down to the cover in my hands. She rolled her eyes dismissively. 'If I was in charge before this, I would have never allowed you to shoot Lara Bingle,' she drawled. My stomach dropped, realising

that this put a whole new kind of pressure on this cover. If it was a dud, as everyone seemed sure it would be, I was in trouble.

But that cover ended up being an iconic *Elle* moment, showing our cover star—who went on to shoot many more covers for us and other fashion magazines over the years—in all her beautiful vulnerability, perched precariously on a rock dressed like a delicate bird in feathery Chanel and introducing a transformed, fully blossomed Lara, with a new iconic haircut, to the cultural landscape. My new publisher, of course, could not have been prouder that her first cover since taking over *Elle* was such a roaring success. She'd known it all along.

THAT MOTHERFUCKING JUGGLE

AS A WRITER on a glossy magazine, you do lots of interviews—with celebrities, It-girls, beauty experts, fashion designers, the wives of former AFL players launching self-monikered scented candle brands, all the big guns. Then you become the editor-in-chief and instead of doing the interviews, often you're the interview subject, which can be a weird shift. Mostly you're interviewed by industry journalists who want to gleefully probe any existential dread you might be feeling around your industry's downfall, but it's often also by daytime television hosts who want to know your opinions on new season fashion trends, sometimes for uni assignments if a polite and suitably ego-appeasing student catches you on the first day of your period when you'd rather do literally anything but work and, more often than not, for lifestyle websites wanting to know the all-important stuff, like how you define your style (which for me I can only describe as 'passes the sniff test').

But at some point during my career, once I'd gone from being the asker to the asked, the questions shifted from being about shopping and my hard-hitting thoughts on this year's Emmy gowns to suddenly being all about family and motherhood and specifically 'the juggle'. (I'll continue to be asked about the magazine industry's downfall, except eventually it will be from the point of view of someone who jumped ship just in time, so at least there's that.)

I answer the juggle questions because I get it. I know how much I also want to know about the juggle from women who I perceive to manage it well. We're all looking for whatever help we can get. But, truthfully, there's nothing I loathe more than being asked about that motherfucking juggle.

I don't hate it because of the terminology, because the word 'juggle' makes it sound trivial and fun. I'm too busy with all my juggling to be bothered by semantics. I don't hate it because I'm asked about it so often that my answers have become practised and by rote, as are most of the answers given by everyone asked about it, and that makes me feel guilty and then resentful. Nor do I hate it for all the usual feminist reasons, because fathers are never asked the question—although I do think this is a missed opportunity.

Personally, I'm very interested in hearing how any man with kids manages the juggle, because I'm convinced they do it better than us. Men manage to have both a career and a family but they also manage to have hobbies, activities they carve out real time for and often spend quite a lot of money on, like golf/cycling/surfing/internet porn. Whatever their passion, the point is that

they know how to prioritise time for themselves that involves more than just seven minutes in the bathtub with some Epsom salts and a sheet mask while thinking about their to-do list— and good for them.

Hobbies are important. They make you more interesting. They force you off the relentless human hamster wheel of 'busy'. They're good for our mental health and can be useful aids in such daunting challenges as making adult friends and cutting ourselves off from scrolling aimlessly on Instagram. They're the very definition of self-care. As women we seem to have forgotten how to cultivate them. I used to think I had hobbies, but I was suffering from a common form of hobby confusion. Netflix, for example, is not a hobby, even though I dedicate a lot of my spare time to it. Similarly, although appropriately expensive, Net-a-Porter is not a hobby. Having some friends I see sometimes is not a hobby. The sporadic exercise I need to do these days just to be able to get up from sitting on the floor without involuntarily groaning is definitely not a hobby. Even drinking wine—unless you choose your bottles from Dan Murphy's based on more than how pretty the label is, you outrageous sophisticate—is not a hobby. Once these things are eliminated, it's clear I'm not as well-rounded as I thought I was.

Actual examples of hobbies are things like ceramics or acroyoga, learning to play the double bass or anything discernibly selfish and unproductive that brings pleasure and joy and can help us to feel like a complete human being with more to us than just working and keeping small children alive. What I need to do is

find me one of those—and then take the seven-minute to-do list bath afterwards. A man would.

Mostly I hate being asked about the juggle because the asking implies that balancing a career and a family is a skill, something you can nail and become good at with enough know-how, and that I have some sort of wisdom to impart on the topic. But the only thing I really know about the juggle is this: the juggle cannot be nailed. All those balls will never stay in the air. One of them will always be headed directly for the floor, or sometimes your head, and there is nothing you or I or Sheryl Sandberg or anyone else can do about it. I hate it when women are asked about the juggle because if a woman genuinely feels she has achieved balance the only true answer she can possibly give you is that she is privileged enough to afford outsourced help or is lucky enough to have a partner, parent or other family member available to contribute to the heavy lifting at home. It's not scientifically possible otherwise. But you'll never get that answer. Instead, you'll get life hacks.

There's nothing wrong with life hacks. I *love* life hacks. I want to know exactly how you pre-freeze your breakfast smoothie packs and which app you use to track your period. I want to know what you put in school lunch boxes that doesn't come home untouched and what supplements you take to stop yourself from falling asleep in a mid-afternoon boardroom meeting because you were up with a baby who didn't sleep until 4 am, after which you remained wide awake with all your thoughts right up until your alarm went off when suddenly you could barely keep your eyes open. (Jks, we all know there's no vitamin that can unfuck your body clock once you've had kids.) I know that in getting

148

through my days over the past fifteen years as a working mother with four kids, I have somehow become a living, breathing life hack. But no woman ever reached the pinnacle of her career and thought that she ultimately owed it all to having a well-stocked gender-neutral emergency birthday present drawer, as undeniably handy as that would be.

The real ways we manage the juggle are a lot less interesting and less helpful than all those life hacks would have you believe. We do it by saying yes now and working out how later. We do it by being a bit crap at everything but knowing that the getting it done is what matters. We do it by sometimes being a bit of a shit friend and an even more shit daughter and sister but usually making up for it with a bunch of flowers or a good D&M just in the nick of time. We do it, if we're lucky, by having some people around us whose job it is to make us appear more in control than we really are and others who value us enough to let lots of things slide. We do it by no longer knowing anything about music or books or any of the things that we used to care about so much, the things that made us as much ourselves as a fancy job title and beloved children ever could.

We do it by being very open to cutting corners, especially when it comes to cleaning our houses, and by lowering our standards for personal grooming dramatically and hoping to god that our partners are too tired themselves to notice. We do it by not judging ourselves too harshly and mostly ignoring that little inner voice in our heads that likes to whisper guilty nothings in our ears. (We've always known she was an arsehole.) We do it by dropping off our toddlers to daycare even if we suspect they might have

pinkeye, and by pretending we don't see the missed call from the school sick bay until we just finish this One Last Thing. We do it by racing home late from work because of a last-minute meeting scheduled for 5 pm by a childless man and then artistically placing five pieces of leftover penne, a packet of sultanas, one boiled egg, one bocconcini ball and half a cucumber, not even sliced, on a cheese board for your kid's dinner and calling it 'antipasto'. We do it by sometimes letting our children sleep in their clothes for the next morning, not always caring if they have a bath, and changing all the clocks in the house to say it's later than it really is so they'll believe us when we put them to bed half an hour earlier at the end of a long day (that one might be just me).

Sometimes I'm better at keeping it together than other times. Sometimes I feel like I've really worked it all out, that I know what I'm doing, that we are a well-oiled machine and my children are kind, well-rounded, whole food only-fed credits to my parenting and, gosh, in those moments, I am really quite delighted with myself. Inevitably, ten seconds after having this smug thought, I'll find a nit on someone's head. More often than I want to admit, that head will be mine. (There is truly not much that can bring you back down to earth with more of a thud than when the celebrity hairdresser in your fancy salon tells you they'll need to take you to the private VIP room to finish doing your hair, not because of your impressive social standing but because, as the stylist whispers dramatically in your ear, *you have lice*.) This is the point where it tends to spiral and before I know it

I'm crying in the supermarket because they're all out of Jamie Oliver fish fingers.

~

There was an exact moment when I realised that whatever juggling skills I thought I had were a complete farce. My third-born, Scout, had just started at a new kindergarten and had become an A-grade leg clinger. One of his brothers had been up sick during the night and had fallen asleep in my bed, so I'd had one of those non-sleeps where your subconscious knows that it might be woken any minute by someone else's vomit on your pillow. By the time I woke up, I already knew I was going to be late for a huge presentation in the office even if the morning ran smoothly, which it no doubt would not. I called my mum to come over for backup, dressed myself rapidly in the dark so as to not wake the sick child, sent another son on his way, got to the school in record time and walk-ran a howling four-year-old to the classroom, his arms wrapped so tightly around my legs that he pushed my skirt up and flashed my granny pants to the Year 4s playing handball. I'm afraid their scars could take years to heal.

By the time I peeled him off joint by joint and managed to place him on the floor with the rest of his class, I was a bit frazzled, mildly sweating and slightly off balance in my brand new Celine boots, which had come off second-best to the turf on the walk in. It was then that I felt an officious tap on my shoulder. It was the Class Parent, one of my greatest fears in life.

'Hi,' she said in the loudest whisper she could manage, cocking her head to one side, struggling to effectively disguise the delight

in her eyes behind a façade of conspiratorial concern. 'I'm sorry, but I think your skirt is on inside out.'

I looked down. I was wearing a Tome skirt that skimmed my ankles, a sheer Stella McCartney ruffle blouse and those grass-stained Celine boots. As on most days, the look I'd deemed appropriate for my activities during work hours was incongruous with one that would work in the school playground at 8 am. 'Oh, it's supposed to be like that,' I explained, fingering the raw edges of the skirt and, frankly, feeling a little embarrassed for her. Class Parent looked sceptical. 'I don't think so,' she murmured. She paused for effect. 'The zipper's on the *outside*.' She didn't sound altogether unhappy about this. I felt behind me. The zipper *was* on the outside. All fifteen centimetres of it. So was the label.

Suddenly I was surrounded by a hum of activewear-clad mothers, well-meaning but visibly wondering where my life had gone so wrong. It was like being in a scene from *Big Little Lies*, but the only thing getting pushed off a balcony was my dignity. 'I just thought I mustn't understand fashion anymore,' one of the other mums said, sounding relieved. 'I couldn't even work out how you got it on,' piped up another.

I would never again feel smug about my ability to hold it all together. In their eyes, I could all too clearly see, I was the woman who hadn't once made the Wednesday morning 'mum chai' after drop-off because I was always running off to my important job in fashion, yet couldn't even manage to dress myself properly in the morning. The silver lining was that everyone felt so sorry for me afterwards that I became the pity parent, the one they all took it upon themselves to helpfully message to make sure I

knew about every mufti day, assembly and class music perform-ance for the rest of the year. Let me tell you, I took that useful, condescending compassion and I ran with it.

That experience only exacerbated my fear of the schoolyard. I will happily spout my irrelevant thoughts on a stage in front of hundreds of people or present my ideas to a boardroom full of intimidating suits who don't understand what I do or why they're expected to pay for it. I have faced childbirth squarely in the face four times and only half of those times have I screamed for ALL THE DRUGS. I have had Fraxel. Hell, I've even been known to strip down to my knickers in an open change room in front of all my peers at a Celine sample sale with barely a heart palpi-tation. But put me in a courtyard of asphalt with some witch's hats stacked in a corner and I'll immediately regress into the shy, insecure schoolgirl version of myself that I once was.

Primary school playgrounds intimidate me to my core and fill me with a churning dread—the way the other mums are always congregated together in tribes, confidently taking everyone in with eagle eyes, brazenly calling the teachers by their first names, whispering school gossip in a language I barely under-stand, knowing all the social rules I have never learned because I'm not there often enough. Even now, four kids down, it takes a lot to get me to enter school grounds. One of my children pretty much has to be getting an award, and it can't just be for partici-pation. I love my children deeply, I care very much about their happiness and their education, but that doesn't mean I don't also thank the universe every day for the invention of Kiss and Drop.

Another occasion, not long after skirt-gate, I drove barefoot as usual into the office one morning, not realising until I parked the car and looked over at the empty passenger seat where my shoes usually lived while I drove that they were in fact not there and that I was going to have to walk through the dingy carpark, cross an inner-city road, enter through the busy lobby and travel up to my floor in front of all my colleagues unshod. The worst part was that this was not even the first time this had happened. That's what the juggle really looks like, and there's no life hack on this earth that can help me.

PART THREE

heart

FORTY

'I DON'T CARE about turning forty,' I told anyone willing to listen (mostly myself). And it was true. I'd distracted myself by planning a debaucherous party in a castle and finding the perfect outfit to wear to it. A lot rides on an outfit for a significant birthday. On a night when the number of candles on your cake is first and foremost in everyone's mind, your outfit must prove to everyone—especially yourself—that you're not Too Old, but it also mustn't look like you're trying too hard to not look Too Old. It's a delicate balancing act.

I had no idea what this perfect not too old/not trying too hard outfit would be until one day when I made a spontaneous last-minute visit to Barneys after a shoot in New York. As my fashion director and I ascended the escalator, we saw on a mannequin right in front of us the fullest, frothiest, tulle skirt a grown woman who always secretly wanted to be Peaches 'n Cream Barbie could ever have dreamt of. It was a dirty pink, dip-dyed Dries Van Noten and everything I wanted without even knowing it. I wore

it with a T-shirt and no shoes to the party but, even better, in years to come I'd occasionally wear it to unpack the dishwasher on a Wednesday and there's not a single time when it hasn't made me feel better about life.

The party was an unmitigated success. There were friends and fireworks and a giant champagne tower, all the best birthday clichés. I partied until dawn in a tiara and at one point my ten-year-old played 'Happy Birthday' on a grand piano as I sat on top of it and cut a gigantic, lavish Nutella chocolate cake covered in lashings of meringue.

And then there was the comedown. Lasting not just a few days, which would be the expected low after such a rollicking high, but for weeks. Then months. *Turning* forty might not have bothered me, but once I was actually *in* my forties—even just a little bit in—I was plagued by the slowly building realisation that I was halfway through my life, that you only get one of them, and that when it came right down to it, I wasn't living my truest truth.

~

Trading your authenticity in exchange for safety, no matter how well intentioned, has a way of eating you up from the inside out, but I didn't know that yet. For the longest time, it had been easy to ignore the reality of my situation. I had a perfectly good husband, as far as husbands went. I'd married him because he was a kind, faithful, good man, and in my extensive dating experience—and it was *extensive*—those had appeared to be in short supply. But a partner's innate goodness is not going to be enough to sustain a fulfilling marriage when you're missing all the magic bits, like

romance and sexual chemistry and compatibility. We didn't really have anything in common. He was sensible and practical, liked making his bed in the morning and watching sport and investing his money for a rainy day. I was a romantic daydreamer who left a trail of clothes from the front door to the sofa every afternoon when I came home from work and spent stupid amounts of money on useless things like decorative cushions and truffle oil I'd forget to ever use. He was stoic and emotionally reserved; I have always had way more feelings than I've known what to do with. These obvious differences in character were summed up as early as our first Christmas together. He was nervous about what to get me and begged for a hint. Not at all helpfully, I simply said, 'Something delightful, nothing practical.' A week later, he told me he was done; he'd nailed the brief. Christmas Day rolled around. I gave him a bicycle. It was black with tan leather details and he was sweet about it but I could tell he thought it was a bit hipster and way too pretentious. He gave me—wait for it—a pizza maker, a photo scanner, a bluetooth for my car and (in a really interesting gift choice for a receiver whose idea of water sports was drinking a pina colada in the shallow end of a pool) an underwater video camera. I know I sound horribly ungrateful—and probably something of a fool because I still use the pizza maker to this day whereas that wanky bike was likely sold on Gumtree long ago—but looking back at that moment it was clear that we had always spoken different languages.

I must have known it then but by that stage I'd already long stopped listening to my gut about such matters. After all, I'd gone with it once and look how that had worked out for me. Instead,

I listened to my head, to platitudes like 'opposites attract' and 'love the one you're with', and to my nanna, who always told me that the key to a happy marriage is to make sure you pick a nice man, just like she did. I took her advice to heart. She was married to my pa, one of the all-time nice men, for more than sixty years. By this stage she was dying and I wanted so badly to hold on to her by emulating what they had, so when I found my own nice man, I married him. Nanna and I just both forgot to take into account the fact that she and Pa were also the great love and passion of each other's lives, the kind of #couplegoals who still held hands and smooched adorably every second that they could, right up until the day that he died. It wasn't his niceness that made their marriage so strong or her so happy. It was their love, their profound connection. You can't emulate that just by wanting it.

Still, our relationship wasn't all bad. We rarely argued, we were pleasant to each other, we had fun. Despite our differences we made a good team—we just probably should have applied to be contestants on *The Block* rather than getting married. For a long time I could easily ignore the rest because his job meant he only spent a few nights a week in our family home and I was busy working and filling the increasingly gnawing, empty hole I was feeling inside with children and friends and, more literally, with lemon drizzle cake. (The main way I've always kept my excess feelings under control is by eating them.)

Part of me suspected the problem might just be me, because no-one else I knew was as much of a relationship fuck-up as I seemed to be. I was surrounded by irritatingly blissful-seeming

marriages (conveniently forgetting through the lens of wanting that no-one ever knows the truth about a relationship except the people who are in it) so I tried my best to ignore the heart pangs I felt when I saw a friend's husband do something as minor as touch his wife affectionately on the arm or a couple give each other a pash at the end of the night when they thought no-one was looking. I carefully looked away when I saw other married people look like they just really *enjoyed* each other's company. I put that sort of relationship down to one of those things that just wasn't for me, like a childhood pony or a burnt orange Birkin. That didn't stop me from aching for it. But leaving never entered my mind. To have one ex I shared children with was unfortunate, to have two would just have been careless. Instead, I told myself that no couple is perfect and I tried very hard to avoid dwelling on my life choices or watching Nicholas Sparks movies.

I tried to keep all my emotions—my ever-growing loneliness, my yearning for a deeper connection—shoved deep inside me, but slowly they seeped out, an annoying trickle at first but pretty soon a full flood. The little voice inside my head that had sometimes whispered to me out of the blue during dinner or lying in bed that *this isn't right* eventually turned into one that screamed it at me, constantly.

I should have ended it much sooner than I did, but I wasn't brave enough. First I pretended it was okay, because I was afraid and I thought what I had should be enough. Then there was a period when I cried and pleaded a lot, unfairly begging him to help me fix things that couldn't really be fixed because they

were never even intact in the first place. Then I slowly just let us become more and more detached from each other, less and less married in any real sense of the word, until eventually (and maybe inevitably) the time came when I fell in love with someone else. It was the coward's way out, but I'd been being cowardly in matters of the heart for a long time by then.

~

Here's a newsflash: the break-up of a marriage can be quite the shitshow, even when you're the instigator. Mine was protracted and painful in ways I could have never imagined. People took sides, even when they didn't realise it. There were times I felt betrayed and misunderstood and abandoned by the people I cared about most in the world, which was almost more hurtful than the actual divorce. There were days I literally ended up on my knees, broken by the process, by the guilt, scared for my future, unable to see where it could all possibly end.

But, as turning forty had taught me, you only get one life. I didn't like what was happening but I also knew I couldn't *not* do it, no matter what anyone else thought. I had a responsibility to myself, in my one life, to at least try to be happy. And for that matter, so did he—while mine was more insistent, I knew I couldn't have been the only one whose inner voice had a lot to say in that relationship. Once I finally determined to forge a new path for myself, to make my decisions from a place of truth instead of from a place of fear, however uncomfortable that might be, however much people might not like me for it, I never once questioned that it was the right thing to do. Even when I was

balls deep in the worst of it, a heaviness was lifting from my heart, and in my darkest moments I felt more alive than I had in years.

~

It wasn't just my marriage I started to see through this new 'one life' lens. My work situation was becoming more and more untenable. But it would take me longer to break up with my job, maybe because I'd only been married for five years, while I'd been wed to my work—or at least the idea of it—for more than twenty. From the very first day I walked into the building as a wide-eyed fourteen-year-old, the seat I now sat in had literally been my only goal. That ambitious teenager had had a very clear vision of what she wanted from her life, and against all odds she had bloody gone and done it. But I wasn't fourteen anymore, no matter what my Netflix history indicated. I was forty, and, like many women my age and in my situation, I was quickly realising that what I'd been focused on with such tunnel vision all that time didn't quite work for me now that I had it.

According to my iPhone calendar—because it was all a blur to me—I'd been on twelve long-haul flights in nine months. That was a lot of bedtime stories missed in the name of fashion. My eldest son's birthday fell each year during Paris Fashion Week and the days of me being able to trick him into thinking it was two weeks earlier or later were long gone now that he'd gone and worked out how calendars worked. I'd been doggedly determined to have it all, but frankly, I couldn't remember what it was to not be tired nor what it felt like to live without a low-level panic that one of my Hermès balls could drop at any time.

While I still loved my job, the company's new owners, the German-based Bauer Media, struggled to understand the intricacies of running a fashion magazine. They were used to celebrity weeklies, cheap to produce and with revenue coming from copy sales. A fashion magazine is an altogether different beast, expensive to produce and with revenue coming from advertising. They failed to get why we would spend so much money on a product that had such few sales comparative to a *TV Week* or the like. But *TV Week* doesn't have to navigate the complexities of four major luxury jewellery houses who all need their ads to be positioned in the inside front-cover spread of the December issue and absolutely cannot run one after another. The clothing *TV Week* shoots isn't a one-off sample that has been flown in from Hong Kong for twenty-four hours so you can take its picture, they don't have to get twelve high-fashion shots in half a day out of Emily Ratajkowski while her new husband keeps trying to touch her boobs on set and, unlike advertisers, their readers don't need to be regularly air kissed and sent flowers to entice them to keep the magazine afloat. I'm not saying that the weeklies don't have challenges of their own (in fact, they're even more cut-throat than fashion mags in many ways). They're just different operations.

Our new bosses questioned why we needed to shoot our own fashion pages and not just syndicate them from, say, a Polish fashion magazine that they also owned, complete with Polish brands unavailable in Australia. Once, when *Elle*'s sister magazine *Harper's Bazaar* ran a Terry Richardson image of Miranda Kerr on their cover (before the Me Too movement, when magazines still used Terry Richardson), one of the revolving-door CEOs asked me

in all earnestness why, with Miranda being Australian and all, they didn't just get a staff photographer—who normally photograph beauty products and vitamin tubs—to take the shot. They proposed that rather than having local writers create our own original stories, we instead source content directly from existing German publications and Google-translate them into English. They suggested that since we all had different audiences, we re-run that same Google-translated story in *all* our magazines, from the *Australian Women's Weekly* to *Belle* to *Cosmopolitan*. They slashed our budgets down to a quarter of what we'd started with and I was forced to go to more and more extreme lengths in the name of producing the magazine to the quality that was expected of the masthead, including having to humiliatingly go out and beg for advertisers to pay for just about everything we wanted to do beyond just getting to print. We started to refer to our place of work as Dunder Mifflin Magazines—a million miles away from the glamorous company of the Packer days that I had been so desperate to work at, where creativity and a rogue spirit were valued, women were empowered to make editorial decisions for products made for other women and brave moves were rewarded. It broke my heart that I was spending half my life working for a company that didn't share my values or seem to care about the product we made for them, half my life that I could have been spending writing screenplays or rewatching *Mad Men* or raising my kids in actual person.

I'd once had the hope that I'd live out my career at *Elle*, spend decades there making a product that I loved and then ride off into the editorial sunset, surviving on nothing but a lifetime's

worth of frequent flyer points and the joy of past seasons' designer handbags. That idea was long gone. As the year went on, I felt more and more like I was dancing on the podium for an audience of none in the very last days of the magazine disco. After twenty-five years in mags, and ten as an editor, I knew the end was coming. I could feel it. I just didn't know how or when.

PLUS ÇA CHANGE

'HAVE YOU EVER done anything dodgy with a jar of peanut butter and a labrador?' I asked the long-haired guy with the big grin at the after party. He pondered the question carefully and stated, 'Yes, probably.' It wasn't a confessional (if it had been, I obviously would have run like the wind) but a new game I'd just been taught, called Deviant Guess Who?. It's just like normal Guess Who?—and uses the original game trays and faces—except, instead of boring, superficial questions like 'Do you have a moustache?' or 'Are you wearing glasses?', the questions are darker, more open to interpretation. 'Do you own a MAGA hat?' is an easy one to get you warmed up. 'Are you likely to have the body parts of missing people in your deep freeze?' is a different angle. An affirmative answer to 'Will an established female investigative journalist one day make a true crime podcast about something you've done and gotten away with until now?' knocks down surprisingly few heads.

It's amazing how just knowing what you want (or don't want) gives you the clarity to recognise when that right thing is in front of you. After a lifetime of falling into long-term relationships with people because they just happened to be in front of me and up for it, I now knew that I was no longer willing to settle for anything other than a Big Love: a proper, earth-shattering connection with a side of deep compatibility. And if I didn't find that, I was beginning to understand—finally!—that alone would be just fine. I had three delightful children and after they left home I could always get a Bernese mountain dog for company. But during that game of Deviant Guess Who?, I got the sense that I might not need the Bernese after all.

I was playing the game with one of my best friend's husband's best friends—take a moment to work that out if you need to—someone I'd always thought of as lovely and funny in a best friend's husband's best friend way but had never thought of romantically (because I never knew what I wanted). He explained the Deviant Guess Who? rules to me and we started playing. I'd watched enough *Law & Order: SVU* throughout my life to be impressively good at it, and at some point while working out if Charles or Emily could be closeted S & M doms, we experienced a Moment. It was almost a physical jolt, like a smack to the face that made me suddenly see *lovely* and *funny* in a whole new light. I didn't know what it meant yet but, eventually, everything that was good in my life I'd be able to trace back to that very second, during that very game of Deviant Guess Who?.

I knew from very early on with Hayden that I'd finally met the man I was always meant to be with—my best ever company,

my person to the end. And, while I knew that some people would roll their eyes and think *Here we go again*, I felt like my history made me *more* qualified to know when I'd found the right thing, not less. It was a bit like the first time you go to Europe and eat a tomato. All your life you've eaten tomatoes, thinking tomatoes were pretty tasty. And then you dig into that first Greek salad in Mykonos or that panzanella in Florence and it hits you that *that's* what tomatoes are meant to taste like? *HOLY SHIT.*

If I'd only ever eaten wondrous tomatoes from the beginning I'd have nothing to compare them to, but all those other tomatoes I'd been eating my whole life up until that moment only meant I recognised the wonder of that real-deal Euro tomato even more. Hayden was my wondrous Greek tomato. He's not happy with this analogy but, fuck it, he's stuck with me now.

~

Having Hayden around might have calmed my heartache, but in my work life there was still a deranged voice running through my head, saying, *You get one life. You get one life. You get one life.* And did I want to be spending mine arguing with a finance person-cum-publisher about what the word 'runway' meant on the cover? Probably not.

I was sitting at the hairdresser's when I got the first call. It was my colleague, *Harper's Bazaar* editor-in-chief Kellie Hush, telling me she was about to resign. We'd both been talking about doing it for months, but she had been quietly working on her exit strategy behind the scenes while I was just doing a lot of really dramatic sighing. Now she was ready, but I was not, not quite.

I hung up from her feeling a little more edgy than I usually like to be while getting a head massage at the basin. I wasn't sure what would happen as a result of her departure or how it was going to affect me, but I knew it would.

Almost instantly, the phone rang again. This time it was a former boss of mine telling me he thought he might have a job for me—a move out of magazines into custom publishing. We agreed to speak the following week. The timing felt portentous. Something started to stir.

I hung up from him and almost instantly the phone rang again. Thankfully, by this point my balayage was well and truly done.

The woman on that third call was my eleventh publisher in ten years, but she was one of the good ones. She was smart and impressive and female, and while those three qualities combined sound like they should probably have been givens for anyone holding the position of publisher of three of the biggest women's magazines in the country (*Elle*, *Bazaar* and *Cosmopolitan*), let me tell you from experience, they were not.

Publisher #11 was offering me a promotion, sort of—the editorial directorship of both *Elle* and *Bazaar*. On the surface, it seemed like a sweet offer, a bobby-dazzler on the CV, not to mention an opportunity to guide the strategy of two beloved fashion titles from a position of more power. I had zero ambition to be a publisher and spend my life drowning in spreadsheets. I liked editing, working with creatives, getting my hands dirty on shoots. Up until then, that meant I didn't really have any career goals left, except hopefully an early retirement, but what

she was offering was an alternative, a middle ground. And if not that, then what?

The offer—of course—came with a caveat. I would have to merge the *Elle* and *Bazaar* teams into one, and cut the staff budget dramatically, making about half of the combined team redundant. It felt a bit like a doctor telling you that you could have that new baby you'd been longing for, but you just needed to decide which of your existing children to give up in order for it to happen. I'd launched *Elle*, hand-picking every single staff member, many of whom I'd worked with for years before that. Three of my former assistants were still on the team—I had been their first boss before they went off to do amazing things else-where only to eventually end up back with me in their dream roles on their dream mag. They were talented, hardworking, dedicated young women who—as with everyone in magazines—had been busting their arses off for years with very little financial reward (unless you count a significant Matchesfashion discount as financial reward, which to be honest, kind of does count when you earn minimum wage, pay Sydney rent and were expected to show up to work every day looking permanently ready for your street-style moment) or respect from the company that employed them. They were my family.

Not to mention that we'd already lived through years of slashes—rounds of redundancies, people who'd quit and weren't replaced, entire support departments that had vanished overnight leaving the editorial teams to take on the work they'd been doing. Despite Kellie's parting quote that '*Bazaar* is a luxury magazine that can't be published on the smell of an oily rag, and I'd like

to finish my tenure while that rag still smells like Chanel No 5', like most of the magazine industry at that point, we'd actually been deep in oily-rag territory for a long time, surviving on just the barest whiff of perfume lingering in the air, like a beautiful woman who has long left the room. The changes they wanted me to implement would have brought down our costs but I felt sure they were almost guaranteed to lock us into a slow bleed until our eventual, inevitable deaths. And my big fear was that I'd be right there at the helm of both, known forever as the editor who closed the Australian versions of not one but two of the most prestigious fashion mastheads in the world. Forget the devil wearing Prada, I'd be the grim reaper in Chloé, and after twenty years in publishing, that was not what I wanted for my legacy.

I stood on the precipice, and I leapt.

JUST A GIRL, STANDING IN FRONT OF SOME OTHER GIRLS, ASKING THEM TO LOVE HER

IN A ROMANTIC comedy, when the two leads come across each other for the very first time, it's called a meet-cute. As filmgoers, we're well trained to recognise a meet-cute when we see one. There'll be a whacky scenario—an orange juice spill, perhaps, or another accident of some kind. There might be a memorable line ('I carried a watermelon!') and if the director really doesn't want to leave the audience with any confusion as to whether this is the meet-cute or not, there'll be a look—a precognitive moment of recognition between the two protagonists, and that way we can be absolutely sure that the wedding planner and her client or the prime minister and his new housemaid or the movie star and the nerdy journalist will end up together by the end of the movie. This makes life easy. You know what's coming next.

Meets don't happen so cute in real life. You aren't given any warning when you've met a person who will play a significant role in your years to come. I have had a couple of movie-style

moments, but they tended to be with temporary romances—the holiday kind, not the serious ones. None of my important relationships have started with a meet-cute; rather, they've started over a boring, expected moment—an introduction at a dinner or a flirty hello at the bar in a pub. Even then, you'd expect there to be some sort of lightning flash, a shudder that runs through your body or brain the first moment you come across someone who is destined to change your life in some big, momentous way. Orchestras should play, animals should howl, *something*.

When I first met Hayden—years before we were romantically jolted over that game of Deviant Guess Who?—I was a bridesmaid and he was a groomsman at the wedding of each of our best friends. That was a scenario that had real movie potential, particularly if we'd hated each other on sight: *classic* meet-cute. But at the time he was in a relationship and, probably more significantly, I was married and had just given birth to a baby five days earlier (yes, I am an excellent and dedicated friend, thank you for noticing). My milk had just come in that morning, my boobs hit my chin and my strapless dress was itching like a motherfucker, so it's not really surprising that we didn't have any kind of spark, let alone hear orchestral music. If truth be told, I don't even really remember him from that night (I mean, I was distracted) and he only remembers my boobs and not in a sexy way. It would have made a pretty weird premise for a movie.

Historically, I'm more likely to have a meet-cute with a girlfriend than a romantic partner. Unlike my husband, who is still friends with all his mates from high school, I didn't make my lifelong best friends until my early twenties, and I remember as

clearly as in any rom-com the moments that I met each of the women who have gone on to play the biggest roles in my life. The first time I ever saw my friend Bron, I was doing the Bondi to Bronte cliff walk. As I turned a corner around the cliff face, I saw a girl with a full face of make-up running towards me, wearing a bedazzled Bonds singlet, earlobes stretched low with enormous chandelier earrings, a huge bag flapping rhythmically at her shoulder and fantastically big, bouncy hair flying behind her. I can't be sure but I think she might have even been wearing heels. In my head, she is coming towards me in slo-mo, and, however she was shod, it was a *lot* for exercising at 10 am on a Sunday morning. I was instantly intrigued. The friend I was walking with told me she was the new beauty editor at *Cosmopolitan* and I knew immediately that I couldn't wait to get to know this jingly, jangly hot mess.

Bron—who I learned not long after was actually a very elegant human and not usually given to running in heels nor bedazzling—contradicts some of my version of this event and has a reasonable explanation for the rest. And while it's possible that she is correct, I prefer to think that on the day that we were destined to cross paths for the first time, something just made her feel the urge to be a little bit *extra*.

My friend Zoë claims our meet-cute started with me telling her that I didn't have any room for new friends, but I refute this. If she is right, one of the smartest decisions a jerk like me ever made was to find the space for her despite my bad attitude. Amanda was introduced to me as part of a hiring process. 'We don't think you'll like this one but just meet with her anyway,'

said the HR woman right before Amanda walked in the room. Amanda spoke maybe three sentences before I knew I was in love with her, deeply and completely, and always would be.

A lot of my other girlfriends I met all at once, in a sort of soul sister meet-cute bonanza. When I was first dating the boy who would go on to be the father of my first two children, he had a very tight group of mates. They lived together, surfed together, worked together, travelled together—they were a unit, one that reeked of salt water, surfboard wax and astounding amounts of male cocksureness. Just after we started seeing each other, I met all of the other guys' girlfriends for the very first time at their annual Christmas lunch. Some of the girls were already close friends and some were newbies, like me, but essentially we were in the boys' world, mere satellites gravitating around a planet of their making.

Surely there had to have been an orchestra playing very faintly in the background that day, because I can recall in perfectly framed movie-scene detail in my head the first time I saw each of these women, heard the first words each of them said to me and formed my first opinions of them. I remember thinking that I couldn't believe anyone as hot as Julz could be as funny as she was, and that Kelly was maybe the kindest person I'd ever met and Jamie the most wonderfully weird and unique. I remember being mesmerised by every single thing Sheree was wearing and recognising that Jen felt immediately like home. And my first-impression radar must have been pretty good because I still think all those things about each of them today. Mostly, I remember thinking

very clearly, before we'd even really made any sort of connection but on vibe alone, that I'd found my people.

Over the next decade, about half of the romantic relationships within this group broke up, including mine. The boys themselves drifted apart—still good friends, but not the inseparable dude mass they had been in their younger days. But that group of girlfriends, along with a few additional ones picked up along the way, just got tighter, until over the years things evolved to the point that we were no longer the satellites but the gravity itself.

At some point, as life got busier and started to take us in all different directions, we started a monthly lunch. The only rule was that it had to be on a Friday, because everything's more fun when you're supposed to be working. We shortened the name to Munch—not our best work, but the idea itself was excellent. Once a month, we'd all wag work for a girls' day. No-one had to be reminded, dates didn't have to be negotiated. If you could go, you went, and if you couldn't, you didn't—but everyone nearly always did. We'd start out pretty and civilised at whatever restaurant was new and cool at that time, and stay so long that we'd either be kicked out or need to order dinner as well, usually ending the night by dancing on a table in a bar or around someone's lounge room.

Women tend to be really good at putting themselves last, at prioritising work and kids and our families and partners (and our partner's family and that thing we promised we'd do for the second cousins of the people who used to live across the road from us four years ago) over our own fun. Making Munch an assumed and regular diary entry made it actually happen.

Since Munch began, careers have taken off, businesses have been started, babies have been born. When we met, none of us were mothers. Now we have twenty-eight children between eleven of us. *Twenty-eight!* The monthly structure ultimately fell by the wayside, as did the lunch part, replaced with a more haphazard mix of Friday night group family dinners, schoolyard catch-ups and stolen minutes wherever we could get them. We've raised our children together (the ones you didn't birth biologically call you their 'spirit aunty') and through it all—the good times and the bad, the fallings in love, the weddings, the pregnancies, the break-ups, the breakdowns, the thirtieths and then the fortieths (which are *much* better parties, by the way), the celebrations and irritations, both major and minor—we've become the truest definition of family.

The first Christmas Munch was a low-key affair, pizza at someone's house. For the second Christmas, we decided to take it up a notch with a costume theme. The theme we went with was 'dress as your mother'—god knows why. An events company had offered me the free services of a nude waiter, one of those weird things that happens when you work in magazines. These two elements gave things an added frisson. Between Julz thinking it was a hoot to keep dropping her fork so the poor naked waiter had to keep squatting to pick it up and the rest of us spending a lot of time looking at the ceiling when having our glasses refilled and wishing we'd thought to bring Glen 20, we decided that dress-up was our jam, and so it has remained, although now on steroids, each year crazier than the last. We've had the Garden of Munch, which opened us up to all the plastic flora Lincraft has

to offer and the simple joys of a hot glue gun; Barbie Munch, complete with life-sized boxes to pose for photos in; Bollymunch, where we looked resplendent in our saris but found it challenging to go to the toilet; and Aerobics Munch Style, the most comfortable Munch ever, and also the one featuring the most camel toes. Our most recent theme was Best of the Met Munch, where the homemade costumes—I wore fifty metres of pink tulle wrapped around me accordion style and held together with a series of tacks that threatened to expose my flesh coloured double Spanx at any moment—could have almost got us in the door at the real thing. It's still hosted in someone's house each year, having learned early that a good lounge room dance floor and an on-the-night social media ban are key to the best and loosest times. We still end up dancing on tables, but in other ways we have matured. We don't order pizza anymore, for example, having moved on to caterers, silver cutlery and chic-styled table settings. We flash our boobs a lot less often in the photos (twenty-eight kids, you see). And these days, it goes without saying, we do prefer our waiters wearing pants.

GOOD MEN

I'M NOT ONE of those perfect mothers. I'm not a great cook, and I'm particularly awful at packing lunches. I've only ever been a chaperone parent at one of my children's school excursions once in my life. Sometimes I get bored and zone out midway through those long stories kids tell that go 'and then . . . and then . . . and then . . .', and just start doing something else, like I've forgotten they were even in the room with me. My laundering abilities are middling at best. We can all agree that there's definitely room for improvement.

But the only part of parenting I really care about being any good at is the raising of Good Men, the kind who love and respect women, passionate believers in anti-sexism and radical equality. I think it's my duty to bring up boys who think that girls are *interesting* and who know that even though they might not understand some of the things they're into, like bullet journalling or Zayn Malik, that doesn't mean those things must be crap or unimportant or not to be valued, no matter what society

and their less evolved mates might say. I want them to know that girls are not objects, they are *incredible*.

Because being a girl and, eventually, a woman—a descriptor I can only asume society decides you're worthy of at around the age of sixty-two, as it still hasn't happened to me—really can be glorious. We get female friendships and glitter eyeshadow and the full gamut of emotions to feel, sometimes all within the one hour. We do better at school and university than boys and have been proven to make more innovative CEOs. We come with boobs, which are universally agreed to be excellent, and spectacular communication skills and we're really good at making things, like açai bowls and human beings.

But my determination to raise my boys to be empathetic soldiers for the female cause is necessary because being one has its downsides too. Things like period pain, having to pay more for pink razors, having to pay at all for tampons, years of wondering if we are or are not perimenopausal and dealing with men sometimes being sexually aggressive dickheads towards us. That last one is a real killer.

We learn so early on as young women that this sort of harassment is just a part of life, so much so that, until recently, we were all pretty much numbed to it—considering it just another unfortunate pay-off of being a girl, the list of which also includes the still-growing gender pay gap, inconveniently timed menstrual leakage and societal pressure to have perfectly harmless hair ripped from our bodies by the roots. I hope this has changed in the aftermath of the Me Too movement, but the experience is so routine, so woven into the everyday fabric of being a woman, that the

idea of a world where it stops being the norm in just a few short years seems desperately optimistic.

~

Sex can be wonderful, life-affirming and momentous. It can be forgettable and mediocre. It can be complicated and messy and weird. I'm a fully grown woman with a high tolerance for small talk, so by now I've had most of the kinds. I once dated, for the course of his Australian tour, a Canadian musician who used to let out a huge roar, like a lion, every time he came. The first time was a real shock. During subsequent times—yes, there were subsequent times, which says a lot about how much a fest-ival triple-A pass can blind a woman in her early twenties with a Penny Lane fixation to all kinds of disagreeableness—I'd just try to squish my ears against the pillow to protect my eardrums and concentrate very hard on thinking about what I was about to order from room service. Later, I'd regale my girlfriends with the story and shake my head, wondering what the hell I'd been thinking, but the feeling was one of mildly mortified amusement rather than any real regret.

But there were other moments too, darker and not so enter-taining to relay to my friends the next day. For years I lumped them in with the sex that was weird and the sex that was funny in hindsight, the sex that was semi-regretful and the sex that was just crap. But these other moments weren't nearly as simple as those and they'd left me feeling not just sexual remorse, but . . . something else. I wasn't sure what because I'd never really let myself unpack any of it. I just knew there were things that had

happened, to me and to lots of girls—*most* girls—that we walked away from with our souls a little less intact than before. The moments were there in my repressed memories, just a low hum rumbling from beneath the tapestry of my other experiences. But it was only as an adult woman in a rapidly wakening time that I was coming to recognise those moments for what they actually were and not just *things that boys do* or *shit that happens to girls*.

I knew I couldn't be alone in having as many of those moments as I did. It wasn't something I'd ever really talked about in gory detail with my girlfriends, but we all knew the stories were there. It was acknowledged in the way we'd discreetly congregate around a colleague on a Friday night if a guy started acting like a pest in a bar or in the way we'd automatically text each other the location of a first date with someone new. In the way we'd quietly catch each other's eyes across a boardroom table when an inappropriate comment was made in a meeting and in the way we innately knew what we 'shouldn't' wear to a place where women would be in the minority. We knew it every time we told a man making a move on us that we had a boyfriend when we didn't, instinctively aware that thinking a woman is the property of another man is more of a deterrent to most guys, not even just the aggressive jerks, than hearing the plain truth that a woman could possibly know her own mind and just not be interested in him.

I'd been trying to work out how we could start that conversation in the pages of *Elle*, but my complicated feelings about my own experiences made it difficult for me to open up a dialogue on a national platform. Was something assault if it didn't hurt?

Was it harassment if I wasn't overtly traumatised by it? What if I wasn't even particularly outraged or affected long term?

And then the Me Too movement happened and a light—a whole fucking chandelier, in fact—turned on in my head. Suddenly I saw my own experiences, as well as those of nearly every other woman I knew, through a new lens. And the more I understood, the more memories came back to me—a myriad of small and not-so-small encounters I'd walked away from and rarely let myself give another thought to, but that had clearly wedged themselves deeply in my soul, ready to bubble to the surface when I least expected it, playing themselves out in current relationships and causing all kinds of subconscious havoc. The movement might have started with the stories of Hollywood rape, but there's been a real power born from the light it's shone on the small, pervasive, everyday injustices women had been experiencing forever and had sort of gotten used to—but have finally decided are unacceptable.

There were all those times in Year 5 when I almost vomited from anxiety before being forced to take my turn in the delight-fully named game of 'Frigid', which involved the boys putting their palms flat on the girls' feet and progressively moving them up our legs, inch by inch, towards our Rainbow Brite knickers. The goal was to let them go as far as you could without squirming or pushing them away. But, of course, even at that tender age, we all knew that the real goal was to find that fine line between being brave enough to not be called frigid, but not so brave that they could call you a slut. Oh, they teach us young.

There was the time at a party of my mum's when a neighbour in his twenties put his hand on my thirteen-year-old bottom while

we were both standing behind the kitchen counter and no-one could see it. His hand seemed to linger for an interminable length of time while I stood still, frozen with fear, conflicted because until that point I'd had a latent, mooning crush on him. I never spoke about it but I was terrified of being left at home alone afterwards, until he eventually moved house six months later.

There was the time during my interning stint in the wardrobe department of the TV show *E Street* when one of the crew members 'took a shine' to me. In my naive, egotistical teenage brain, I thought I'd made a cool, older friend, never wondering what a thirty-something-year-old man could have possibly found to be mates with in a fifteen-year-old schoolgirl. Sometimes on the weekend, he took me to lunch in fancy restaurants like Rockpool, where he talked to me about my future career and delighted in introducing me to things my little suburban brain had never heard of before, like shiitake mushrooms and grooming. (The latter, of course, only dawning on me years later.) At some point, he invited me to a party at his house. I arrived to an extravagant picnic in the backyard, complete with—and excuse me while adult me vomits in my mouth a little bit—champagne and oysters. I was the only guest. Nothing happened, and I was so creeped out by the situation that I never spent any time with him again. But thankfully I'd decided a career in television wasn't for me because I never felt comfortable going back to *E Street* either.

There was the time at age sixteen when I passed out from too much Malibu and pineapple juice watching a movie at the house of a boy I knew as a friend and woke up topless, with his hand on my breast and his tongue in my mouth. I freaked out

and start crying, he blamed me for being a tease and complained that he'd bought me the Malibu for nothing. I ran all the way home, rigid with shame, feeling absolutely culpable, and never said a word about it to anyone.

There was the time not long after that when I found out my supposedly sweet, sensitive boyfriend of six months—who I thought I was deeply in love with and who I thought was deeply in love with me—was breaking up with me when his drunk friends called me from a party and took turns describing our fairly wholesome sexual encounters back to me in lurid detail, each offering to pick up where he'd left off, while I listened to him laughing in the background. I don't know what it feels like to be a victim of revenge porn, but I can only imagine that this was the pre-camera phone version, every bit as horrible and humiliating and violating.

There was the time at seventeen when I'd been out with my family at a local community event and went home early with a headache. Unbeknown to me, I was followed back there by someone a few years older who I only vaguely knew. He talked his way in, tried to kiss me, then pushed me into my bedroom and onto the bed. I remember kicking and screaming, I remember his weight trapping me underneath him, the feelings of panic and terror as we struggled and the relief when he finally just gave up and left. Once it was over, I didn't ever let myself think that I was almost raped, although that's absolutely what I'd been sure was going to happen to me at the time. I didn't get angry about it or call the police, or even my mum. Instead, I was embarrassed about it, like it must have been all my fault, and I blocked it out, never to speak of it to a soul.

I didn't even remember the incident until decades later.

There was the time at my first big overnight advertiser conference as the newly appointed editor of *Shop* magazine when the general manager of an important beauty brand walked up to the lunch table where I was sitting anxiously with the entire executive team from my company, trying desperately to do my best impression of a professional grown-up, and told me I was 'playing with the big boys now'. When I asked him what to expect, he shrugged and quipped, 'Oh, I don't know . . . blow jobs?' It was an attempt at a joke, made in a different time, but it still made me burn hot inside with smallness and humiliation while everyone in the room laughed, even the other women. Even me.

There was the time I received a phone call, only a few years back, from a much, much older man who had once been my boss and who I had always considered a mentor. We chatted about my work for a while and just as we were about to get off the phone, he asked me, 'Would you ever consider, Justine, on a lovely day like today, perhaps spending it with me?' I didn't react for a moment. I had a sense of what he meant, of course, but I was also desperately hoping that there was an innocent meaning behind the comment. He'd sold his business a few years earlier and a little part of me was praying he was just bored and looking for company. I didn't need to worry about there being any confusion. He filled the silence bluntly and devastatingly. 'Do you know what I mean by that, Justine? I mean, in a bed.'

So, not a lot of room for interpretation.

Did I call him out for propositioning me when I'd never given him any indication that I was open for our relationship to move

in that direction? Did I slam the phone down, letting him know in no uncertain terms how offended I was, how cheap it made me feel, the sense of loss I experienced when I realised that someone I'd almost worshipped for his guidance and role in my career had possibly always just seen me as a potential piece of arse to unceremoniously cheat on his wife with on the next sunny day he found himself at a loose end?

Nah, of course not. What I did was laugh awkwardly and make some quip about being happily married and then got off the phone as fast as I could, but not before sweetly promising to call him back if I ever changed my mind, like he was a telemarketer I felt sorry for. And then I cried, although I didn't quite know why. And then I turned it into some kind of 'Men, amiright?' anecdote to be pulled out after a few negronis with the girls.

I'm a grown woman. Unlike Weinstein or Cosby or Epstein or nearly all the other public faces of this exposé of male sexual entitlement, this man no longer held any economic or professional power over me. I was not being threatened physically by him. And it was just a phone call. He was essentially, in some misguided way, asking for consent. When he didn't get it, he went away and I never heard from him again. Still, my reaction felt so spineless, so apologetic, so almost-complicit that I felt sickened by it afterwards and for a long time to come. Still, it has sat somewhere tight in my chest ever since, even though my brain has told itself time and time again that it was nothing, although I know it wasn't—even by the law, which defines sexual harassment as any unwelcome sexual behaviour that makes a person feel offended, humiliated or intimidated, which it definitely did.

~

I'm just one woman and these are just a sliver of my experiences, no better or worse or more awful than any other woman's. In fact, they're so par for the course, they're almost mundane. But they illustrate so clearly what we do—what we've been doing forever—in the face of our common experiences of sexual assault, objectification, harassment and violence. We ignore them, trivialise them or turn them into a joke. We block it out, handle it, keep it a secret or shrug it off like the Cool Girls we think we should be. We tell ourselves it wasn't 'real' assault, we blame ourselves or—worse—we blame each other. For the longest time, we normalised this sort of behaviour to the point that unless it was violent vaginal penetration by a stranger in a dark alley, we refused to recognise it for what it was. Even when it was removing our bras while we slept off too many Malibus.

I didn't have a father around when I was growing up, and in the years before the clarity the movement and the sisterhood gave me, when I was still trying to piece together my own experiences, I'd often wondered if that had played a role in how many tales like this I had to tell. I was wild and impetuous and had a single mother who was full of love, but the distractions of keeping a young family fed and sheltered by herself allowed me a long leash when I probably needed a really, really short one. Not only to help me avoid troubling situations with men and boys, but to stop me from accepting dares that had me jumping onto fast-moving trains, taking thirteen car sickness tablets at Carols by Candlelight for kicks in Year 9 and then tripping on

them for two whole days at school, and spending most Thursday nights in Year 11 when I claimed to be studying at a friend's house dancing on tables at Kinselas in Taylor Square. The fact that I'm even alive to this day, let alone a responsible, recycling mother of four, should be a shock to us all. I'm sure it is to the mothers of the girls who worried that I was a bad influence on their daughters in high school. But you don't have to be fatherless or impulsive to have racked up a litany of stories just like mine. You just have to be female.

For all the dark moments, I've also had a million—well, maybe not quite a million but, you know, *up there*—wonderful, positive experiences with men. Men who were respectful and kind, supportive and considerate. Men who made grand gestures and who cried while watching *Atonement*. These are the kind I know it's my duty to raise.

I do this by gently indoctrinating my sons with feminism at every possible opportunity and preaching consent and acceptance and intimacy and equality as soon as they realise they have penises and, thus, privilege—so, from about three days after birth. I may not ever get to see a daughter walk down the aisle, but I'm outrageously confident that I'll get to see four boys be really great partners and fathers, supporters and defenders of my kind till the end. I might be a bit lax when it comes to cooking them gourmet dinners and their school shirts may be very rarely (never) ironed, but when it comes to turning my boys into warriors for women, fighting the perils of a misogynist society, I am Mother of the Year.

ONCE UPON A CO-PARENT

I TWIRLED THE best tagliolini al tartufo of my life around my fork as the Russian editor—older, louder, larger-than-life—waved her wineglass around, regaling the table. I'd survived another full day at Milan Fashion Week with just a handful of almonds stashed in my bag for sustenance and I'd been looking forward to this meal at Ristorante Da Giacomo all day, so I wasn't going to stop eating for anything. (This Alba truffle pasta, the generous aperitivo at the Bulgari Hotel and the famed savoury panzerotti—like pizza doughnuts—from Luini were my go-tos in the city, making it a biannual challenge to still fit into my borrowed designer samples by the time the Paris leg of fashion month rolled around eight days later.) But I listened, rapt, through heavenly mouthfuls as she informed me, conclusively, that every woman should have no less than three husbands. She ticked them off on her fingers, heavy with Cartier jewels.

'One is for babies—for pretty babies, you need pretty husband,' she explained. 'Two is for money'—she gave a little *c'est la vie*

shrug, like a girl's gotta do what a girl's gotta do. 'Three is for companionship,' she continued, matter of factly. Then she looked at me with a delightfully wicked glint in her eye. 'And four is just bonus for me because I'm so special!'

Luckily for me and Hayden, I don't feel I'm nearly as special as that. But I'm almost up there.

~

When most people talk about 'having it all', the 'all' is referring to a great job, a functional family, a nice house and possibly a few pieces of old Celine in their wardrobes. The 'all' generally doesn't refer to 'all the baby daddies'. I've ended up with three and that's just one of the ways in which I've gotten this 'having it all' malarky wrong. This one significant miscalculation has unfortunately led to other errors in 'having it all', including 'all the double-barrelled surnames' and 'all the school holidays scheduling'. Also, 'all the awkward explanations'. I'm at peace with my life choices, although when I do need to mention it, I generally ensure to drop into the conversation that I'm in good company, with both Kates Winslet and Hudson also on their third partners, and they both seem like perfectly respectable women.

When I first joined this exclusive yet in no way aspirational club, I felt supremely confident in my ability to handle it. There are not many things I can say I'm really good at—the skills that I do have tend to be those that are really useful in life, but no good for showing off. I'm good at sleeping on planes and my ability to wake up exactly on time without an alarm in any circumstance is uncanny. I'm better than any concierge at holiday planning.

I can peel a prawn with impressive speed and dexterity, a talent born from growing up in a family with too many mouths and never quite enough to go around. And I always thought I was exceptionally good at co-parenting.

When my first partner and I broke up, we shared the rearing of a one-year-old and a three-year-old. For a while, until they started preschool and we lived too far apart to make it feasible, we'd split the weeks in half. At first, I found the days the boys were at his house unbearably painful. I'd never felt so alone. In the space where normally there'd be two raucous toddlers running around, the sudden silence was deafening: no sound louder than a million tiny Lego pieces not being played with. But soon I started to use the time to my benefit. I won't go so far as to say I ever really enjoyed it, but it definitely had a silver lining: I could work back late, catch up with friends, add to my sleep bank, go to the bathroom in blissful solitude. Eventually, I even dated. And I could have sex! With a real, live person!

I got all that stuff done in those three days a week so that my time with the boys was uninterrupted by having a life of any other kind. It made me a better, more focused parent when I did have them. Eventually, it seemed obvious to me that if only all couples lived with shared parenting rules—where each one had their predetermined, allocated time to do what they needed to do, to be themselves in the way that they had been before they'd had kids (without all the point-keeping and tit for tat that usually accompanies these things between couples), not to mention the financial independence and separate bathrooms such an arrangement would bring—many more marriages would stay together.

In the meantime, the boys' dad and I were the very model of modern co-parenting. We made all the kid decisions together and celebrated birthdays and milestones as a family. He came over if one of them was ever sick to help carry the burden, I sent them off to his family Christmas with presents for all his people. We had the occasional family dinner after drop-off, helped the boys make the other affectionate Mother's Day and Father's Day cards, continued to share all the friends we'd had as a couple. One time, we even pulled off a co-holiday to Bali, where I took them for the first week, he arrived halfway through and we shared a couple of crossover days all together, then he brought them home a few days after I left. We even discussed co-writing a book about co-parenting, so smug were we in our abilities to get it perfectly right.

Of course, we had our moments. Disagreements about dates, tensions about money, awkward moments when new relationships began. But these were fleeting. In general, our children knew their parents were mates, that we both loved them and—in our own way—each other.

I just assumed my second attempt at co-parenting would be as smooth, but I was wrong. As it turned out, the singular reason my first partner and I were able to co-parent so well was not because we were especially evolved or consciously uncoupled, like I'd thought, but because we had been able to break up so easily. It happened quickly—just a fight, really, that took on a life of its own, between two people who were never as into each other as we were into our kids. We broke up before we had time to really injure one another, with no time to build resentment or animosity. We were young and we owned nothing, so there

was nothing to wrestle over. We weren't married, so there was no divorce. Things didn't have the chance to get ugly in the way that only talking through lawyers can make happen.

Divorce is a harrowing experience for everyone involved, even the people just watching from the sidelines. If these things could be measured, I suppose I was much more heartbroken by my first break-up, and we had more children to navigate the rearing of, which should have made things harder, but just going through the motions of divorce draws things out, makes things be said that can't be unsaid or unheard. It's one sucker punch after another, almost always.

If the first time around I could boast that our break-up was better and more carefully navigated than our relationship as a couple was, I can categorically say that, second time around, my ex's and my divorce was much worse than our marriage had ever been.

My first break-up was a private pain. I could control my own narrative. As I packed my mum's car to follow the removalist to my new apartment, I decided that I'd give myself a week to hate him and then I'd let it go, move on and treat him as what he was: someone I'd have to know and deal with for *the rest of my days*. That's a pretty long time. But before I'd made it out of the street, I realised there was no point in my scheduled week of rage. At some point I was going to have to work out how to navigate this new world, and that may as well be sooner rather than later. Plus, I was moving quite far away so if he wasn't nearby to hear me cursing his name under my breath or see me shooting wounded daggers in his direction, then the only person suffering

for the next seven days would be me (and maybe my new neighbours). And for the most part—not including days when I had PMS or when we argued over Christmas plans or he just really, really pissed me off, as people in our circumstances are going to do sometimes—that's how it played out.

Not the next time. The next time it felt like our break-up belonged to everyone else but me. It belonged to family law firms and accountants and mediators and friends and people we barely knew who treated our lives like it was gossip fodder or some kind of personal injury or affront to their values. Half the time it felt like an out-of-body experience, like I was hovering above watching what was once my life get smashed to pieces in ways I had no control over. Other times, I was the sledgehammer.

Afterwards it came as a shock to me to realise that I wasn't actually the incredibly evolved child sharer that I thought I'd been all those previous years. That my navigation skills in that arena had been no more than the luck of a set of conditions that had made it easy. That under a different set of conditions, I was as crap at this as any other human being out there trying and failing to maturely share parental responsibilities with someone you once shared a life with but would now cross the street to avoid if you thought you could get away with it.

The second time around, I'm not proud to say, there were no shared birthdays or tag-teamed holidays, no funny photoshopped cards. Instead, there were big grievances stemming from small, imagined insults, petty withholdings and chilly drop-offs. Divorce brought out the worst in us, as it does with almost everyone except Jennifer Garner, Hollywood's living saint.

Sometimes the underlying grudges felt like they were never going anywhere. Where my first ex and I were similar and could always connect over a book or a movie we both loved, while we could relate as fellow writers and magazine editors when we needed to lighten the heaviness of daily co-parenting operations, my second ex and I had none of those common threads and that made things harder.

We assumed our son—at this stage still in preschool—was unawares, because ours was a silent war, played out mostly via passive aggressive emails and texts, but I knew that he would have never expected a day out or a shared visit to a sushi train with both his father and me, that he automatically anticipated two birthday celebrations for himself and acted silly and awkward when he had to say goodbye to one of us in front of the other one, so on some level he must have known all along. Worse, he had already, all on his own, learned to navigate it—and that broke my heart.

~

I might not be the expert kid sharer I thought I was, but I have learned some stuff along the way. Navigating parenting after divorce is all about selective recall. You need to actively choose to remember the qualities of a person that once made you decide that procreating with them was a reasonable, sensible, maybe even a thrilling idea. Concurrently, you need to actively choose to forget literally everything that happened from the very first time you noticed exactly how loud they breathed until the day they walked out the door with the stupidly expensive smart TV

you never even wanted in the first place but the removal of which you still inexplicably resent. If you really, really want to be the most evolved co-parent you can be, you need to practise radical kindness even when it makes you bristle (never has the saying 'do unto others' been truer than when your ex asks you to have the kids on their night because they have a hot date and can't find a babysitter). You need to consciously assume your ex only has the best intentions and never, ever try to read between the lines, because if you weren't able to read each other's minds when you were married and living together you probably won't be much good at it now. You need to take responsibility for your half of the shit from when you were married, no matter how much their transgressions loom large in your head. And you need to see them as they are now—just another parent in the world doing the best they can—rather than persist on seeing them as they were then. They were in an unhappy relationship, remember, and that doesn't bring out anyone's finest self. Of course, you won't do any of this. Not at first. But you can work on it day by day, if you just live by the golden rule: What Would Jennifer Garner Do?

For us, things are getting better. Small but significant chess moves are made. Lately, there's been a casual 'x' at the end of a text message about swimming lessons. An enthusiastic exclamation pointed 'Thanks!' when a photo is sent or some small favour is granted. Things are becoming unfraught in a way that seemed unimaginable when we started this. I'll be good at it again, eventually. I have to be, it's one of my only skills.

LOVED

HAYDEN EXPLODED INTO all our lives like a giant confetti cannon, like waking up to the smell of your birthday cake baking in the oven, like when 'Livin' on a Prayer' comes on the radio just at the right time for a spontaneous road trip singalong. It took me a while to get there, but I finally ended up with the love I'd always thought was something that belonged to other people, but never me. Unexpectedly, the boys felt exactly the same way. They loved him on sight. He was the missing piece of the jigsaw puzzle, not just for me, but for them too.

When we met, Hayden was a single guy living in inner-city Melbourne, working hard and partying six nights a week. He was free as a bird, the most fun human on the planet. Then, within months of us falling in love, this guy who had been all about the good times moved to the beachy suburban outskirts of Sydney and jumped headfirst into being stepdad to three boys aged between three and eleven.

But, somehow, he is great at parenting, a better parent than any biological parent I've known, including myself, and I'm only slightly sorry to say that all of my boys would probably agree. In our house, he's the one who packs the lunches, knows what days the excursions are, remembers to return the library books and picks up the cardboard for the art projects without being reminded. He has boundless energy, an innate ability to find the celebration in anything and a natural skill for asking the right questions and bringing out the best in small people. He understands all their pop culture references and has all the in-jokes. He's firm when necessary and affectionate all the time. He has better parenting instincts than me, but in my defence, he's also not as tired as I am and that definitely helps. I've been parenting for a third of my life. That's a lot. Some days I might even say that it's too much.

However, despite thinking previously that my uterus was well and truly closed for business, and despite him repeatedly saying that he loved the boys so much he didn't feel like he was missing out on anything, I couldn't help feeling like it was crazy that someone happy to give so much of himself to raising children would never raise one that was completely his own. It also felt wrong that, given all the little people I'd made with other people, I wouldn't be making one with the great love of my life. So we decided to try for a baby. I was a bit nervous for me and my geriatric womb, but I was also aware that I might never have to face up to that worry. I was forty-one. 'There are no guarantees,' I told him. 'It could take months,' I told him. 'It might never happen.'

I fell pregnant immediately.

After the shock wore off, it felt just like riding a bike. I told myself not to be blasé, this fourth time around, because it was Hayden's first experience of making a baby and I didn't want to steal the wonder of it from him. But I had no need of the warning. Being pregnant felt different this time, in this relationship, with this man. He made every moment special, every hundredth wake for the loo in the middle of the night, every gnawingly familiar wave of nausea—it was all magic, because it was all with him.

Ten weeks into the pregnancy, I was at an important lunch with the CMO of the fashion brand Coach who was visiting Sydney from New York. I was in the good mood that I always was when carbs and business collided. Then suddenly, sitting there at the table over entrees and small talk, I felt a sensation between my legs—that feeling you get when you realise your period has just come. *Strange*, I thought, *but probably nothing*. It was my fourth trip to the rodeo and I was past the point of needing to google every odd twinge and mysterious bodily function. I excused myself discreetly and went to the bathroom. There was blood on my knickers. My heart immediately lurched, but I couldn't think of an excuse to leave the meeting without making it a big deal so I went back to the table and sat down. But the wetness increased through lunch. And then I started to feel some mild cramping. That's when I got scared.

By the time we got to coffee, I was pretty sure something was really wrong. I carefully stood up at the end of the lunch and held myself together as we air kissed goodbye, a process that seemed to take an interminably long time. I saw our international guests into a cab and turned to my deputy editor, who didn't yet

know that I was pregnant, and said to her as quietly and calmly as I could that I couldn't return with her to the office because I thought I might be having a miscarriage.

I jumped in a taxi to St Vincent's, the nearest hospital. Hayden was away working in Melbourne and as I sat in the A&E, the only non-junkie in the room, I called to tell him what was going on. Hearing his voice made me feel better and I started to feel more confident that it was going to be okay. So many of my friends had struggled to fall pregnant or carry babies to term, but I was a relentless breeder. *This*, I kept repeating to myself, *is probably nothing.*

I sat in the waiting room for over an hour. In that time, the bleeding and cramping stopped, just like when you go to the doctor and as soon as you get there your fever drops or your cough stops and you know they must think you're a crazy hypochondriac or just looking for a doctor's certificate so you can get yourself a four-day weekend. I started to feel like I'd overreacted, and I was annoyed with myself because now I wouldn't be able to make it to school pick-up and I'd have to call a girlfriend to do it for me. I was taken into an observation room where a nurse came to take down all my details. And I waited, more and more sure with every passing minute that it would all be for nothing.

The doctor eventually came around and sent me for an ultrasound. Feeling more confident by then, I even had a little flutter of excitement to be getting a bonus look at the baby out of what seemed sure to be a redundant hospital visit. But then the operator wasn't very chatty, which took the wind out of my sails a bit. Worse, she didn't seem to know what she was looking at and

asked weird, upsetting questions, like, 'Are you sure you're pregnant?' and 'Was it confirmed by ultrasound?' I've been known to hold a grudge and that woman and her bedside manner do not want to come across me in a dark alley at night.

I was sent to wait in an emergency department bed with my meth-head roommates from the waiting room. An hour passed, then another. Things started to feel ominous. I was exhausted—I still had a long drive ahead of me to get home, whenever that would be—but I was scared to shut my eyes in case one of my new friends was planning to steal my shoes.

Finally, the doctor came to tell me that while it wasn't his area of expertise, in his view the pregnancy was no longer viable. He suspected that I'd had a missed abortion, which meant that the embryo died days earlier but hadn't begun to be expelled until now. The phrase felt accusatory, like he was blaming my body for being somehow inattentive, too distracted to notice something as big a deal as its baby dying.

I finally knew then that it wasn't nothing, that what was happening was definitely something.

The doctor booked me into the early pregnancy clinic at a hospital closer to my home in two days' time and sent me on my merry way. Nine hours after walking in the door, I put on my shoes (thankfully still in my possession despite a suspected microsleep), picked up my bag and walked out. It felt somewhat unceremonious, but also appropriately depressing, to be standing out the front of a hospital alone in the middle of the night waiting for an Uber to take me back to my car after finding out about such a Big Thing.

Hayden flew straight home and two days later we were sitting together in another hospital waiting room, one where the junkies had been replaced by couples in various stages of sadness. I hadn't imagined that I'd miss my roommates from St Vincent's, but I did. I missed how I felt around them—optimistic, naive, *pregnant*. I was given another ultrasound, this time by someone who was much more sensitive, but still confirmed the worst. Because I could only go on a stand-by list for a D & C and the bleeding meant that things were already underway, we chose to take the drug to move things along and allow my body to go through the process by itself at home. We organised for the boys to be kept occupied for the weekend, filled up a trolley with all the d'Affinois, Kettle Chips and Cadbury Dairy Milk we could carry and went home to have ourselves a miscarriage.

I put on my most comfy jammies while Hayden agonised over what music to play. There is no Spontaneous Abortion playlist on Spotify. We both did a lot of googling before I took the meds. Women on miscarriage message boards had written about intense pain, that it was like going through labour. My labours had all been horrific, so this wasn't great news. But at least I could drink pinot noir through this one, which was a small win.

And so we toasted to the baby we never got to meet, and I swallowed the first tablet. Eventually I started to feel some minor cramps. They didn't feel like labour to me, but then maybe other people's labours weren't as awful as mine. Or maybe I had a really high pain threshold. I'd always thought I was kind of a tough cookie.

I went to bed to nap it off. This went on for the entire day. I'd feel some mild pain and think, *Was that it? Is it over now?* but I was never sure. And so we passed the evening slowly, eating all the cheese and watching mindless reality TV and Hayden rubbed my back when the cramps came and went and kept my wheat pack warm. And after each wave of pain, we asked each other, 'Was that it?', never really having any actual idea. I was surprised there could be so much ambiguity over a thing like an embryo expelling from your body. It felt like a thing a woman should recognise.

We were too wired to go to sleep, so we stayed up, sipping Baileys in bed and talking about anything and everything. We played a lot of cards. It was almost like one of those dates when you're first falling in love and don't want to waste any time sleeping, except for the heaviness in the air and the distinct lack of steamy sex.

The following day was more of the same, but that night at least we were tired enough to get some sleep. By then, we were getting used to this limbo state, this strange, quiet bubble— just the two of us (which was rare enough), bunkered down and riding it out together. Despite the cramping and the confusion, it was weirdly beautiful—a gentle, lingering way to say goodbye to the idea of a baby, kinder than it might have been if it had all ended in an emergency room D & C and an Endone haze.

The cramps were worse the next morning. *This is definitely it*, we both thought, as I huddled on the sofa. The pain hit a crescendo, more like a dodgy fish taco than labour, but more than I'd felt over the previous two days, and then it started to subside

until I felt nothing at all. I assumed it was over. That evening, I was supposed to be hosting a panel event for *Elle* in Melbourne which I'd been resisting cancelling, not wanting to let anyone down, and I felt so fine that I contemplated going. In the end, Hayden decided for us both that I was a crazy person and that I couldn't fly (obviously), but we figured a drive would help to shake us from our cabin fever, that strange reverie that felt like it had been going on forever. We also felt like we deserved a little treat so we decided to pop into our favourite plant shop on the way home to buy ourselves a miscarriage present, which is just like a push present, but less annoying and probably not boasted about on Instagram afterwards.

It was as we were leaving the plant shop that I felt something suddenly slide out from between my legs and lodge in my specially purchased miscarriage nanna knickers. I had no idea what it was. It felt enormous and firm and horrific, like my insides were falling out of my body. I froze on the spot, terrified of what would happen if I tried to move. Hayden ran for the car and managed to manoeuvre me into the passenger seat without bending my legs, which was a real challenge, and we found ourselves laughing awkwardly, despite the panic.

At home, we got into the bathroom as quickly as we could and I tentatively pulled down my pants to find something that no-one at the hospital warned me about and that I hadn't read about on any of the message boards either—a bloody mass, as big as a lemon, like something out of a B-grade horror movie or the eighties TV show *V.* I have a strong disposition but I nearly fainted. Hayden turned pale but stayed stoic for my sake. It

seemed too big, and wrong anyway, to flush it down the toilet—the idea of it getting stuck and having to fish it out manually was too much to bear—so I wrapped it gingerly in toilet paper and Hayden took it out of the room. He never told me what he did with it.

Then we went back to our positions on the sofa, where first we sat stunned and silent, processing what we'd seen, and then we cried a little bit, and at some point we started to feel relieved that at least we could finally stop asking, 'Was that it? Is it over now?' Because that thing, whatever it was, was definitely *it*, and it was definitely *over*. So at least now we knew. We put *The Bachelor* back on to take our minds off what had just happened and as we watched the couple on TV attempt get to know each other over a dinner they could only pretend to eat, I thought, for the hundredth time that weekend, how lucky we were to have each other, to be in this life, with all of its ups and downs, together.

~

I once read a story of a couple, Maurice and Maralyn Bailey, whose sailboat was struck by a whale in the Pacific in the 1970s, leaving them to float together in a tiny life raft for 117 days. There were constant storms, the raft got a tear and needed to be reinflated every half hour, and water needed to be bailed out constantly, day and night. Their bodies were weakened, ulcerated from constant exposure to sea water and nutritionally depleted by a diet almost exclusively made up of raw fish and turtles they scooped up from the water surrounding them by hand once they ran out of canned food. Like us, they also played a lot of cards. Before he

died, years later, Maurice described those 117 days stranded at sea with the woman he loved as the best days of his life.

I thought of the Baileys a lot during this time. Their experience was extraordinary, while ours was sadly altogether too commonplace, but now I understood the sentiment of being able to find happiness and solace in any situation with the right person. And looking back, with the comfort of knowing that we would go on to fall pregnant again and that that time it would end with a baby in our arms, I think of those three days as the time in my life that I felt the most love, and loved. It was, as far as these things go, the best miscarriage ever.

TWO DRESSES

I'VE HAD TWO wedding dresses, which is more than you're supposed to have but, if I'm going to be really honest, probably just enough. The first was from Jenny Packham, shipped from London after I tried it on during a trip there and then couldn't stop thinking about it. It was made from metres and metres of delicate ivory French tulle, as light as a feather. It had a low back and a raw hem and it was made to wear while dancing shoeless on a table under a country sky strewn with fairy lights, which I did.

My second was a very different kind of wedding and a very different kind of dress. Hayden and I planned to elope to Texas—that's how much we ship Coach and Tami Taylor's marriage in *Friday Night Lights*. Not that that was the only reason. It was also the first stop on a family road trip around America that we'd been planning, which seemed like as good a time as any to tie the knot. Who doesn't dream of a honeymoon with three kids in tow?

An elopement, particularly a destination elopement, requires a very particular dress, one that suits the location as much as the woman. After endless searching, I finally found the perfect one: a Chloé pre-fall look on Net-a-Porter. It looked exactly right online—a delicate lace bohemian dream worn in the campaign with fringed tan boots peeking out from underneath a handkerchief hemline that pretty much screamed Texan bride, in the least Britney of ways.

Then it arrived and the shape was weird and it sat on my body in a way that a girlfriend described sadly as 'Amish-esque'. There are some Amish communities in Texas but that wasn't the vibe I'd been hoping for. Still, the dress had all the qualities I wanted other than how it looked on me, and just like when you return to the fridge multiple times on work-from-home days hoping that each time you'll discover something delicious in there that wasn't there before, I kept looking in the mirror in the hope this time I'd see something different in the reflection. I stood there for ages, doing the buttons up, undoing them, trying it on with different shoes, piling up my hair in a way I would never wear it—as though an eighties French roll with tendrils would make all the difference—then dropping it despondently when it inevitably wasn't so.

My mother eventually commented that it looked like a maternity dress and had me shove a pillow up the front to prove her point. And suddenly the dress, shapeless and ill-fitting until then, was transformed. Turned out it was a shotgun wedding dream-dress all along, which also felt suspiciously appropriate for Texas. And while no-one in their right mind would ever decide to fall

pregnant just to make the perfect maternity-cum-wedding dress work . . . if the perfect maternity-cum-wedding dress helped to bring forward your *existing* baby-making plans, well, then everybody won.

But now I had a conundrum. The returns policy gave me two weeks to decide to keep or return the dress, which was not a time frame that worked for my ovulation patterns or our trip. Did I keep the dress in a kind of wild optimism about my ability to fall pregnant to plan at forty-two years of age, risking the fact that it could be a financial maternity punt almost in line with a round of IVF, or did I do the sensible thing and return it, hoping that if I was lucky enough to fall pregnant with perfect timing, I'd be able to find it again? Ever the calculated-risk taker (and shopping enabler), I decided to keep the dress, figuring I could always sell it on eBay if things didn't work out. The perfect destination wedding dress was worth a punt.

~

The first time I got married, our engagement fell right at that transition between weddings that were a church ceremony with a party after and weddings as the ultimate form of self-expression and a demonstration of your combined creative force. Possibly in an effort to keep busy and not let myself acknowledge the instinct that surely must have been there somewhere deep inside me that my husband-to-be and I weren't right for each other, I went all-in on the latter. I controlled every last detail, down to getting myself hospitalised before the wedding with a kidney infection caused by a rigid adhesion to the Kate Middleton-approved Dukan diet.

The wedding itself was an explosion of personal touches. His mum made the bunting, my children hand-dyed the paper doily flags. There were cute badges with quirky nicknames directing all 220 of our best friends to their seats and there was a hip menu of the kind of American street food—Mexican corn and pork ribs and truffled mac and cheese—that was big at the time. There was a children's mini glamping area and an open-air whisky bar. There was a custom-made floral bridal arch with artfully woven twigs and an entire garden's worth of hydrangea, a cross made from driftwood and the prerequisite photo booth with a back-drop of streamers that had to be shipped from Portland. *I couldn't possibly have not had the streamers shipped from Portland.* There was karaoke set up in a rose garden, a noted psychic doing love readings, wedding guest bingo with a bottle of Casamigos as the prize and a burger and doughnut delivery at midnight.

It was all so personalised! So detailed! So painstakingly curated! So focused on the wedding instead of the marriage! Later, I'd come to see that there was a reason I cared so much about all those little details, why I spent the speeches not really listening but wondering if the speechmakers were going over their allo-cated time limit. I was trying to fill a hole, providing myself with a distraction from a truth I was refusing to face. But as a party, it really was one for the ages.

My second wedding couldn't have been more different. Hayden and I got married in a pretty wedding chapel outside Austin on the very first day of that family road trip because that was the day we could fit it in around all the barbecue eating we had planned. The only guests were our kids and our mums. We

woke up in the morning, ate a delicious brunch of non-Dukan approved honey butter fried chicken and waffles, then split off to get ready. I organised, sight unseen, a bunch of wildflowers from the nearest florist to be delivered to me at the hotel in the morning, along with a birthday cake from a local bakery that I customised with a few extra blooms from the bouquet. My son, Iggy, walked me down the aisle. The ceremony was short, but full of special moments. Hayden made vows to me but also to the boys, and we did a handfasting ceremony to signify our becoming an official family. We all cried, including the boys and our friends who were watching over brekky at home via FaceTime. Afterwards, on the recommendation of the make-up artist, we went to a honky-tonk bar where the dance floor full of cowboys cleared out for us to have our first dance to a song we definitely did not choose called 'When it's Christmas Time in Texas', the awfulness of which only added to the moment. We had dinner off the menu in a quaint restaurant recommended by a friend of a friend. Nothing about any of it was curated or personalised, and somehow that made the day even more perfect.

As for the dress, I was twenty-six weeks pregnant as I walked down the aisle, filling it out in all the right places, thighs rubbing like mad, oversized pregnancy areolas threatening to expose themselves with every step. It was glorious.

~

We went on to have the trip of our lives, our new family establishing itself more and more with every stop, as my body grew bigger and bigger every day. The baby—growing in a uterus

that was chronically overused and exhausted, under abdominal muscles that were super chill and relaxed—had an 'unstable lie', meaning it flipped positions all the time and was often sideways. (Because of this, it would end up being my first caesarean section of the lot, something that seemed hideously unfair for a fourth time around.) The constant movement, almost freakishly visible from the outside, made it feel like the baby was on the trip with us. When we went hiking in Zion, the boys took turns to push my body up the tougher sections of the hike and surrounded me and the baby protectively when they decided he was getting too close to the more treacherous edges. When we sat in diners playing card games and the classic American board game Sorry! as we waited on our meals, they'd watch my belly to guess which foods made him somersault most impressively under my skin.

Hayden and I had fallen in love over Deviant Guess Who? and as a family we'd been playing games ever since. We start every weekend morning with what we call a 'full set'—a routine of five card games that we play in a strict order over a cup of tea. I've grown into the habit of always keeping a set of cards in my bag, and we've played full sets all over the world, in airports and fancy restaurants, as a way to ignore annoying relatives at family functions, even to decide a winner in a petty argument. If Hayden and I ever have a real argument, proposing a full set is our way of asking to make up, to let the other one know that we've moved on, to silently agree to reconnect. It's the bubble that we build around ourselves as a couple, and a family, even in a room crowded with people. Those five card games are as

much a part of the tapestry of our life together as reality TV and a good Central Otago pinot.

~

Sometimes it's the simplest things that fill you with the most joy. Like being able to say, 'I have a wonderful marriage.' I never imagined in a million years that I would ever be the kind of person who could say that. But here I am, saying it.

BOYS, BOYS, BOYS

IT WAS 1981, peak *Star Wars* and I was in my kindergarten class colouring in yet another picture of Jesus and some lambs when I got called to the office. My aunt was on the phone to tell me that my mum had just given birth to a baby boy. It was a crushing blow. I'd been hoping for a girl. I was going to call her Leia. Instead, I ended up with a Luke. It was my first taste of gender disappointment. It wouldn't be my last.

The next time I experienced anything like it was not so much a gender disappointment as a gender wtf. I was pregnant with my second child. I already had one boy and I didn't care what I was having this time around, but somehow I'd been convinced that I was carrying a girl based purely on the wisdom of every single person I came into contact with. Everyone just seemed so *sure*.

I knew why. According to the old wives' tales, when you're having a boy, you carry 'all belly', but when you're having a girl, you carry 'all over'. Also, girl babies, those tiny, innocent little bitches, supposedly 'steal your looks' and make you appear tired,

which is obviously just another way to pit women against one another right from the womb because who the fuck doesn't look tired when they're making a person and going to the toilet thirty times a night when they should be sleeping? By the time I was standing in the shower in the birth centre, at the pointy end of pushing out a child, I was certain beyond all certainty that this baby was a girl, because I'd essentially spent nine months being told by everyone I knew that I look god-awful. Accepting this, I think, instead of just having it confirmed by ultrasound, was a self-esteem issue.

I've never understood the idea behind waiting for the 'surprise'. Unless you've whipped yourself off to America for sex selection, it's a surprise whenever you find out, at forty weeks or ten. Pregnancy is deathly dull and interminably long, and I highly recommend getting your excitements whenever and as often as you can. With tequila being out of the question and back-to-back *Love Island* episodes almost guaranteed to do bad things to a baby's IQ in utero, finding out the sex at some point during gestation just seems to me to be the logical choice in pregnancy thrills. Also, let's not forget that at the end of the nine months, you get handed an actual live human baby (and soon after that, if you're lucky, a sashimi platter). That day gets to be special enough, and if it's a surprise you want, there's bound to be an episiotomy or haemorrhoids or an emergency C-section in there somewhere that can make all your dreams come true. With my first baby, I'd found out the sex as soon as I could and had loved it. Second time, enough people were telling me, in their roundabout way, that I was fatter and more haggard than I should have been that I

didn't question it. By the end, I had myself truly convinced that I was about to be in possession of a pigeon pair.

Back in the shower, the midwife was squatting on the tiles beneath my naked, heaving form, labour being the gloriously dignified experience that it is. At the final push, she caught the baby and lifted it up behind me to untangle the cord. My then partner looked over my shoulder and—having obviously clocked my girl-making puffy face and widening arse as well—uttered a sentence that perfectly marked this wondrous, transcendent, important moment in all our lives: 'Holy shit, it's got balls!'

I couldn't have cared less if the baby had turned out to be a golden retriever, but I was just not prepared. I'd spent nine unattractive months convinced that my almost-two-year-old son, Milo, was about to have a little sister. It took me a while to get my head around the idea of brothers.

The feeling passed quickly though. I soon learned that sons born close together make life easy. One set of toys, one set of clothing, two little guys born to entertain each other, to play together and, one time, to bite each other on the penis through pyjamas during a particularly heated wrestle. Long story.

The next time, it hit me harder. The next time, I wasn't so nonchalant. The next time, I desperately wanted a girl, for all kinds of complicated reasons.

~

Gender disappointment is a shameful emotion. No-one wants to feel it, let alone acknowledge it. It's ungrateful and offensive to so many people struggling with infertility. It's irrational and

antiquated and confusing. It's also an inaccurate term, because what we're really referring to is disappointment over a baby's biologically determined sex at birth, not their gender, which of course they are free to define—or not—once they're out in the world themselves. However, because 'sex disappointment' just sounds like the Sunday morning experience of most women in their early twenties, I'll stick to the commonly used phrase here for clarity.

Gender disappointment gets a bad rap because everyone assumes that if you want a girl it must be about ribbons and bows and being able to paint the nursery pink, or if you want a boy that it must be to carry on the family name and other such offensive and outdated notions. But in my experience the reasons anyone longs for a child of a particular sex aren't usually so superficial. It might be about hoping to see the physical qualities of your long-deceased dad in a son or being scared of turning into the same sort of hyper-critical mother to a daughter that yours was to you. For me, the third time around, it was very early on in the pregnancy that I realised I'd married the wrong man. It was terrible timing, to suspect you and your husband don't really love each other just as you're preparing to bring a person with your shared DNA into the world. I spent most of the pregnancy depressed and anxious, weighed down by the physical process of what was happening but without feeling any of the magic to counter it that I'd experienced the two times before. I'd lay awake at night, wildly distressed about not feeling the same connection with the baby in my belly as I had in the pregnancies for my two other sons. I was terrified to talk about it with anyone but inside I was constantly worrying about how detached I felt and how much I

was resenting this baby's existence, with the subsequent guilt and fear sending me even further into a downward spiral. That the baby might be the little girl I'd dreamt of raising (Enid Blyton! Learning how to use tampons! Systemic sexism!) was the only light on what looked like a very dark horizon. Most of the time, it felt like my husband and I lived in completely different worlds. I was terrified that I wouldn't know how to raise a little-boy version of him. A girl felt safer, more knowable.

The day of the ultrasound just happened to be my birthday, which to me—ever the optimist—was obviously a sign. We all went along. 'Tell me it's a girl!' I lightheartedly begged the operator, not imagining for a minute that she might not. 'Ha-ha, nope, definitely a boy,' she said, continuing to casually slather my belly in jelly, completely indifferent to the blow she'd just delivered.

I went instantly cold, and not just from the goo. I was told later that I became a lot like Cameron in *Ferris Bueller's Day Off* when his dad's Ferrari smashes through the glass wall and goes over the cliff. I became catatonic. Calls were coming through for my birthday but I couldn't take them. My reply to birthday texts was a cut and pasted 'Baby is a boy! I'll be fine!', which was a sure indication to everyone who received it that I was not fine at all.

I'd realise later, of course, that my reaction had very little to do with the baby's sex and more to do with my general unhappiness, but at the time all I could think about was that I didn't have room in my heart for another boy. *I'm never going to be able to love this baby*, I told myself. The thought sickened me, but I couldn't stop it. None of this was anything I ever voiced

out loud. On the outside, I made jokes about breeding football teams, and on the inside, I loathed myself.

Then one night, late in the pregnancy, I dreamt about the baby. In the dream, he was about eighteen months old. I was putting him into his car seat when he looked at me with eyes much older than even his dream years. He held my face between two pudgy toddler hands and said, clear as Oprah, 'Of course you're going to love me. *I'm your baby.*'

I woke up with a new feeling of clarity. It was such a simple idea—that we love our babies—but one that I'd allowed myself to forget. I was already a mother. I knew that love! I knew how primal it was, how inexplicable, how it hit you like a force. To think it wouldn't conquer all, even in the mess I'd found myself in, was delusional. I was still worried, still hesitant, but I was no longer quite so terrified.

Scout was born after the most epic in my series of epic labours thus far. (I must have the uterine version of an Aman Resort—none of my babies ever want to leave.) In keeping with the person he would soon prove to be, he was never, not for a single second, a sleepy, vague newborn. There's a photo of the moment he was placed in my arms, a tiny face wrapped in a blanket, huge eyes staring into mine with a confronting intensity. In that moment, everything else vanished—the hospital room, the midwives busying themselves with my placenta. For a second, it was just me and him. And he communicated to me with those big eyes just as clearly as he had in the dream—I swear, it was almost audible—'*You love me*', and I knew, in that moment, that I desperately, whole-heartedly did. In fact, despite all my fears, he was the only one

of my babies that I felt that mythical immediate rush of love for that I'd heard about before I had children. With the first two, I'd mostly been exhausted and preoccupied with whether or not it was too soon to ask someone to bring me a cheeseburger, but with him, I was all-in. Immediately. For the first time in months, I felt the fog lift from my heart.

~

The labour had gone on so long that my mum had brought Milo and Iggy, then aged eight and six, to the hospital after school, thinking it would be over when it was still far from it. They'd hung in a corner of the birthing suite for hours playing on an iPad, and when I'd suddenly felt the need to start pushing, it all happened so fast that everyone just forgot about them They'd been so quiet, watching the video for 'Weird Al' Yankovic's 'Fat' over and over. I suppose it was appropriate. Much to my horror, they had ended up witnessing the whole thing.

Once I pulled myself out of my reverie with Scout, I asked them what they'd seen. Milo had learned things and he was delighted to be asked to share: 'I saw a *lot* of hair! And I thought, I didn't know Mum had a hairy bum! But then I realised it was the baby's head . . .' I quickly told him he could stop talking then and maybe not to share that story with any of his friends at school.

Iggy, on the other hand, felt differently. He shrugged, avoiding my eyes. I pushed him for his thoughts and he resisted, then looked up at me with less innocent eyes than a six-year-old should ever have. He took a breath, then spoke.

'I saw you do a poo.'

~

The next time I fell pregnant, I was leaving nothing to chance. This time, there was no deep underlying reasoning behind my craving for a girl—it was *all* superficial. I already had three beautiful, amazing boys, but all my friends had daughters and I was sick of the FOMO. It was my turn for the fun clothes and the pretty bed linen and mani-pedi days and going out for high tea. I don't know why I suddenly thought I was a character in a Nancy Myers film but I wanted my life to include that moment when I sat with my daughter sipping champagne as she chose her wedding dress, and to be the favoured grandmother who got to be in the room for my grandchild's delivery and made my daughter feel inadequate about her ability to raise a child or decorate a house. Of course, I knew that none of this was guaranteed, that I could get a girl who was more into touch football than My Little Pony (and I knew that would actually be so much more awesome), that she could prefer that her mother didn't watch her push a person out of her vagina, or that one of the boys could be the best gay son ever and give me all of the fun clothes anyway. I understood all of this *intellectually*. But the heart wants what the heart wants. And so did everyone else's hearts. Hayden wanted a daughter so that the boys we already had never felt like they'd been replaced by a biological son. Milo, Iggy and Scout all had enough brothers for one lifetime.

In the lead-up to conceiving, I lurked so deep in the various gender-selection forums that I started to feel more familiar and attached to the regular posters there than I was really comfortable

with. Time4ABoy83 and her ilk might not have actually known me, but they *got* me in a way my actual friends couldn't. My IRL friends all had girls, every single one of them, so how could they truly get it? They told me girls were harder, moodier, more complicated, that I was lucky to have the simplicity of all boys. I was a girl once, so I knew this to be true. Regardless, I was doing everything I could, no matter how dubious the science or debunked the theory, to make one.

I tried acidic diets (because boy sperm thrive in an alkaline environment), deprivation diets (because historically more girls are born in times of scarcity), cycle timing (to give the slower girl swimmers time to get to the egg). I tried sex on my period and a single attempt in a cycle without really understanding the theory behind either, and there was a time it's best not to speak about when I soaked one tampon in lime juice and another in yoghurt and . . . well, I don't want to go into details but I can tell you it was not the fun time it might sound like. Finally, I gave up on all the theories and went for the simple science of finger-crossing. The odds there seemed to be as good as anywhere else.

Despite my attempts to take all the joy out of sex as I turned conception into a gigantic lime-douche field experiment, eventually I fell pregnant again, about eight months after the miscarriage. As we waited for the result of the ten-week NIPT test to come through and reveal the baby's gender, I was as calm and reasonable as ever. Jks, I was agitated and likely to bite anyone's head off for any minor cause. But I was also increasingly sure that there couldn't be a world where this didn't happen. All around me,

people were getting full sets with just *two* children. I had given it twice as many goes as that, so I felt good about my chances.

~

I called the clinic the morning the results were due. They were in, they informed me, but had been sent to my GP, who would call me in her own sweet time. This was not a good sign. I'd been her patient for years and I was pretty sure I was as close to being her friend as a person who she gave regular Pap smears to could be. She had lived through this the last time around. She knew how much I wanted it. If she had the results, and they were the right results, she would have called me already.

The hours passed by. We'd been supposed to go to lunch with some friends, but Hayden was resisting. He wasn't sure if we should be out in public when the call came. 'It's our baby,' I scoffed, remembering the lesson I'd learned with Scout. 'It's not like I'll *cry* or anything.'

Finally, at lunch, my phone rang. All the confidence I had drained from my body as I answered. 'Juzzy?' came my GP's hesitant voice. She took a breath. 'You have a very healthy baby . . .'

I burst into tears.

She tried to explain more about the test results but it was hard to communicate through the choking sounds of my ugly-cry. I got off the phone, dried my tears and returned to the table, where our friends valiantly attempted to help celebrate our new baby boy through thinly veiled sympathy (or that's how I saw it, because they had a daughter between their two sons) and we all sat through an awkward lunch where I drank my only glass

of wine since conceiving and pretended to be dealing with the news in a healthy, sane manner.

Then we got in the car. As soon as I was alone with Hayden, who had been doing his best to stoically support me as I completely ruined his entire pregnancy experience, I became hysterical. Off-the-Richter crazy-town. I was wailing, howling, making sounds that were subhuman. The feeling was physical and overwhelming. I scared myself with the intensity of my sadness, ashamed of how I was carrying on, so aware of how many women struggled to even have one baby while I was lucky enough to be carrying my fourth.

But my husband, an annoyingly evolved and emotionally intelligent human, recognised my reaction for what it was: grief. I was grieving for a daughter who'd been so real in my head but who I now knew for sure would never be real in the world. He took me home and put me to bed where I continued to writhe, something inside trying to escape a body that seemed, in my mind, to be playing a relentless bad joke on me.

Then, one by one, my children came home. First Scout, who was so set on having a sister that we couldn't tell him the news until we had it in us to sell it with more conviction, but who brought me a glass of water and wiped my brow, thinking my tears were because I was sick. Then Iggy, who looked stricken, not for himself but for what he knew I was feeling, and who ran straight to the bed to hug me with the special brand of kindness and compassion that I've never known anyone else to be capable of. And then Milo, the teenage boy version of myself, who was comically agape at the news and immediately went into some

awkward jokes that only he and I got, making me laugh and *almost* forget the seething pain that I'd been feeling just moments before. With each of their entrances, I remembered again how much we love our children, how unique they are, how different the connections are that we have with each one. And it reminded me, importantly, that this baby would be his own little person, not just another fucking boy.

I didn't stop being sad right away. I'd still pause in the middle of a conversation about something as benign as needing to do my tax and start crying, gutted anew that I'd never be able to read *Little Women* to anyone. But the longing I had for something I knew I was never going to have became less and less acute. Eventually, I got down to googling 'how often are NIPT tests wrong' only once a week. I stopped obsessing over the fact that I'd never have anyone to talk with about the adventures of *Anne of Green Gables* and instead started working on making sure the boys knew to not let hairs grow out of the mole above my lip when I was too old to spot it myself.

It still upsets me that I won't be the favoured maternal grand-mother, but I'm holding out hope that one of my boys marries an orphan, or perhaps, less darkly, someone whose own mother lives abroad. But not, like, New Zealand, or anywhere else close enough that there's a chance my grandchildren could love them as much as they love me. Very, very far away.

~

A week or so after we found out, the boys sat me down in front of the TV, excited for a family movie they wanted to surprise

me with. It was *Grease 2*, the lesser known, less good sequel, but the one that somehow managed to play a more significant role in my childhood. They watched it with unbridled enthusiasm, only partly bribed by Hayden. Every time one of them went to scoff, they caught themselves and instead would turn to me and say unconvincingly, 'It's not *that* bad!' (Tip: it *is* that bad.) They wanted to prove to me that I could share with them all the things I would have shared with a girl. And it worked. We laughed so hard at the ridiculousness of some of the songs that they made their way into our family lexicon. So although I might never stage-mum my way through a ballet recital, I can sing 'Reproduction' with my tribe of boys in the car anytime I like. It's weird, sure, but until my orphaned daughter-in-law comes along, it's good enough for me.

WHEN LIFE GIVES YOU LICE

I WAS AT a fashion event, minding my own and everyone else's business, when someone impossibly young and impossibly cool asked me—as people tend to do of late, even when they already know the answer—how many children it was that I actually have these days.

It's a question I always find uncomfortable. I'm not quite the Octomum but confessing to four kids in the modern age isn't far off admitting to plans to take on a couple of sister wives and start your own family cult in outback Queensland. People either ask me about it wide-eyed and fascinated, like they truly cannot fathom why anyone would want to ruin their Saturday mornings that way, or sharp-eyed and warily, like they'd better be careful lest I be on the market for just one more sister wife. This was the latter kind.

I answered with the same sheepish shrug I always do, the kind that seems better suited to admitting to eating the last piece of cake or being caught cheating in pub trivia than when

acknowledging the most precious beings in one's life. It made no difference. My fellow party guest, who could really do with a lesson or two in polite small talk, could barely contain his moral horror and asked me something out loud that I'm pretty sure he'd meant to just think inside his head: '*But what about the environment?*'

My first reaction was to be offended, but then I remembered every single plastic dummy, every single bottle I'd misplaced the lid for and had to replace in its entirety, every methane-filled disposable nappy wrapped in a plastic bag that each of my babies had worked their way through—all of it still floating around somewhere on this planet—and I had to nod and agree that, yes, I had well and truly done my part to ruin it for everyone. Mea culpa.

But it could have been worse. I have four children, which is a lot, and no sister wives, which is right, but actually I've been pregnant seven times. Imagine how bad my carbon footprint could have been.

~

The first two times I fell pregnant were when I was young, one in high school and one just a few years later, because I always like to take multiple times to learn from my mistakes. My teenage pregnancy ended in a miscarriage before I'd even processed what was happening to me, the one in my early twenties ended through an abortion. Both times I was scared—although, in hindsight, not nearly scared enough—and remorseful. I was also a little ashamed: the first time because a pregnancy in high school is scandalous, and the second because I knew that having been

through this once, I should have known better. But those feelings only lasted as long as the pregnancies did. Afterwards, I mostly just felt relieved. For something that has the power, maybe more than anything else, to change the entire path of a person's life, it's remarkably easy to course-correct.

I know this is not everyone's experience. I've had some friends who've had abortions and found both the decision and the process harrowing, the way I assumed I would feel before it actually happened. But for others, like me, the experience left no lingering pain or trauma once it was over. It was a dumb thing that happened, that led to a regrettable experience and then a sad period of time. But then it ended. Life moved on.

And not too many years after these first two pregnancies, there would come a time when conception was no longer scandalous or regretful, when peeing on a stick was a moment full of promise instead of dread, when pregnancies led to babies who were brought into the world with joy and excitement and will still change the path of my life, but only for the better. Mostly.

I adore my children but I don't live for parenting. I very much enjoy being their mother, but the whole concept of motherhood as a verb, as a competitive activity, makes me feel horrifically unprepared. I think it's unfair and illogical, not to mention boring. Helicopter parents terrify me. All that hyper-focused attention—it's not natural, I'm sure it endangers the children. Saying that, I'm not completely free-range in my parenting style. I'm strict on things like bedtime and manners and their pop culture choices (we are a proudly Wiggles-free house). Although nits have occupied

an inordinate amount of my leisure time over the past sixteen years, my children aren't utter street urchins.

~

The firstborn, Milo, once took nits with us on holiday to New York. I spent every night of that holiday close to tears, trying and failing to remove them with the only useless plastic comb available in Duane Reade, where the sales assistants nearly jumped out of their skins when I went in asking about head lice treatments, something that wouldn't even raise an eyebrow at home. But no feeble American nit lotion managed to take on our hardcore Australian nits, so we all ended up with them, a family of five scratching our way around the city, living a communal holiday hell and proving that what you see on Instagram is never quite the whole story (#wanderlust).

Nit-smuggling aside, Milo was the one who transformed everything, the one who turned me into this life-defining thing called a mother. He's the one I'm learning it all alongside for the first time, sometimes getting it surprisingly right, hopefully not fucking him up too permanently when I don't.

When I was pregnant with him, I spent hours in bed watching *The Sopranos*, happily dipping whole bananas into jars of Nutella like a spoon and imagining the times we'd share. (These are the indulgent, contented moments you only get in your first pregnancy when you're still allowed to think you and your bump are the centre of the whole world, and they were worth every gram of the thirty-seven kilos I put on. Not that it wasn't still shocking when the baby was born and the ratio of my weight gain worked

out to be 10 per cent child:90 per cent choc-hazelnut spread, but I did enjoy myself.)

I knew what he'd look like, how close we'd be. I had very specific daydreams: one of my favourites was to picture him at about age seven, us cuddled up together on the sofa, drinking cups of weak tea and eating buttered English muffins as we watched *Stand By Me*. I pictured him as a young man—handsome, smart, kind, funny. Before he was even born, I felt like I knew him. I couldn't wait to meet him in the flesh.

And then he arrived and, oh my lord, was he ugly. It took me a second to register that this was my baby, he looked so unlike the gorgeous creature I'd been spending so much time with in my head. Our two-day labour—never has the name been truer—meant he had essentially been born with two heads, one at the front with a face on it, and a whole other full-sized (but thankfully faceless) one at the back. I loved him with all my heart, but he was not the baby I'd spent nine months imagining. Luckily, the redundant twin head eventually went down. He became cute. I can't say I wasn't relieved.

I was the first of all my friends to have a baby, ugly or otherwise. They were all young, still single and dealing with sleepless nights of an altogether different kind. I got into the habit of taking him everywhere I could so I didn't miss out, to day parties and festivals and to dinner with the girls before they'd continue on to a big night. He was the youngest regular at Hugos Pizza.

Maybe because of this adult beginning he's always known exactly who he is and what he thinks, a quality I wish I could say he got from me but definitely cannot. In preschool, he told

me he 'could never imagine having a need for more than one or two really good friends at a time', and even as a teenager he's still someone who prefers a small group to a big party. Another time, at six, he was appalled to hear that I was going to a champagne breakfast. 'Champagne is really more of an after-dark thing,' he declared haughtily, like the meanest of small boy-shaped Mitford sisters. He was wrong then, as in other times, but he can never be told so. That quality he does get from me, as well as many others, more than he'd like to know. He's the closest thing I have to a clone in the world, in the way we think and things we feel. He makes me feel *seen*.

People always told me that when it comes to physical affection, you lose boys at about the age of ten. In my experience so far, that's not completely true. Milo won't get into our bed to watch a movie with the rest of us anymore, but sometimes when we're both sitting on the sofa watching TV, he doesn't instantly move his foot away from mine if it brushes against his, and it makes me secretly giddy, too scared to move in case I bring his attention to it and he whisks himself away into teenage-boy-land again. I'm not allowed in there.

But we're tight, he and I. We're allies. Like me, he's a first-born, so we recognise in each other the embedded sense of duty and guilt, the battle weariness that comes from being a family trailblazer. Second-borns, like his brother, have it easier.

Even second-borns' nits have it easier. The first time Iggy got lice was when he was three. I spotted them in the morning and knew I couldn't send him to daycare, but it happened to be Australian Fashion Week and I had to be at a show, so I popped

a fedora on his head and took him with me to work. While we were there, he was spotted by the US street-style photographer The Sartorialist and ended up being the first Australian featured on his blog. Iggy owned those nits, a perfect embodiment of the perhaps less well-known saying 'when life hands you lice, turn it into likes'.

This is classic second-born stuff. When I was pregnant with him, someone told me that your first child is like marriage, with all the ups and downs of any serious long-term relationship, but that your second is more like a love affair—easier, lighter, less likely to require regular visits to a therapist. If this is the case, and in my experience it is, Iggy was born for the role. He's the lover in the family, the boy who is all heart, who feels big and wounds easily. It's him I turn to when I want to watch a sad movie, and we don't care when the rest of the family, with all their stinky testosterone, laugh at us for how much we blubber.

He's mild-mannered, but in the very best sense of the word. He's not weak, just not bothered by compromise. He wants everyone to be happy. When I told him I was getting divorced, he stayed quiet, then gave me a huge hug and said, 'Whatever makes you happy, Mum. I know you always do the right thing for us.' It hurt my heart, the confidence that a ten-year-old could have in me and my decisions when I had absolutely none at all.

He adores his big brother with a ferociousness that is often taken advantage of, once making a deal to take over Milo's dish-washing nights for a week in exchange for a nightly high-five from him before bed, which is maybe one of the saddest things I've ever heard. I tried to talk him out of it, but he's okay with

vulnerability, and why would I ever want to stop that? He's a living, breathing antidote to toxic masculinity.

As a teenager, he's still okay to have his arm around me in public. He attempts to give his stepdad exactly seventeen kisses every night before bed, some weird in-joke I don't understand but think is sweet. His love language is touch and I think I know why. A couple of weeks after he was born, he got sick with a mysterious eye infection, and he and I spent ten days alone together in the children's ward. It was where I spent my thirtieth birthday, curled up with him permanently attached to my body, starting his life from a single hospital armchair. It wasn't too bad actually. He's always been my favourite company.

But if I thought I was any kind of expert at all in raising children after bringing these two very different boys into the world, I soon worked out that I was sorely mistaken. I never really knew what it was to have children at all until the third came along. Scout is a hurricane, every cliché of a third child: loud, hammy, strong-willed—because third children know they need to be and do more to get attention and to speak louder than anyone else in the room to be heard. His everyday demeanour is less seven-year-old child and more Danny DeVito playing a litigator in a Quentin Tarantino movie.

He's brave and brazen—as are his nits. They once went with him to the dentist, where I first noticed them as he sat in the chair, and then watched on in helpless, shameful horror as they literally crawled across his head, cocky as anything, just millimetres from the hygienist as she leant over his face. But he's also a natural rebel, an independent spirit, a street-smart hustler and

an instinctive performer. All of these qualities combined make him like no-one else I've ever known, adult or child. Plus he's a little guy and has a serious Napoleon complex. How a personality so big can be jammed into a body so tiny is a miracle of physics.

He's different to the rest of us, a frat boy born into a family of nerds. I worry because I never want him to feel like a fish out of water, but I don't need to because he revels in his uniqueness. He's his own man. When we went to Las Vegas on holiday he didn't think it was grubby and gross like the rest of us did. He loved it. We know this because he told us all the time. 'I love Vegas!' he'd declare every few minutes, walking around with his mouth agape and the dollar bill he'd been bribed with to put socks on that morning clutched in his hand, ready for whatever Sin City could throw his way. We passed a Chippendales promo troupe in Old Vegas, semi-formally dressed in just the bottom halves of their tuxedos and bow ties. He was fascinated and wanted to know who they were. Once informed, he immediately added Chippendale to his list of potential occupations—alongside magician, SWAT, jockey and stand-up comedian—because the idea of wearing no shirt every day to work and dancing around to get money thrilled him. What goals.

Raising him can be difficult. First, because it's nigh on impossible to make him do anything he doesn't want to do. Second, because he makes me laugh so much. He's the kind of kid everyone I know without kids loves because he's a living YouTube clip. Everything he says is a punchline. He's Honey Boo Boo and Bart Simpson mixed together with a bit of Joan Rivers. I don't really want him to change because then I'd have

no stories to tell at the office. And third, because he is the third and oh god I am so tired.

Having a little brother has been life-changing for him. Finally, he has someone in the house smaller than he is, with an earlier bedtime than his and who—most importantly—hero-worships him the way he's never been before, the way his Napoleonic hunger for power demands. This unconditional two-way love has made this little hell-man gentler, more vulnerable. He's terrified of something hurting the baby, of someone throwing him too high, of one of us leaving the safety gate open, of him sitting on the floor without being properly penned in by a nest of pillows, every skerrick of visible floor covered in soft padding. I can't imagine what that must be like for the fourth, Odie, growing up being loved so fiercely by someone as fierce as him.

I love Odie desperately but I know nothing of him yet, not in the way I know the others—their ins and outs, quirks and habits. When you have a baby, you think you know them and that you love them as much as you can ever love anything. But now that I've done this a few times, I can say that this is not completely true. Sure, you love a baby to full capacity *now*—but like any relationship, as you get to know a person and build a history of shared moments and experiences, that capacity expands and grows.

So far—and, honestly, in my experience babies do have a tendency to turn out surprisingly like who you think they'll be from the get-go—he's a chubby ball of joy and contentedness. He horrifically got his first case of nits at just three months old, all those grubby boys and their grubby friends trying to hug and kiss him all the time, and he just smiled through it, so I'm guessing

he's pretty mellow and tolerant. That's a relief, because I'm too old to be starting from the beginning with any real gusto again. Milo says he thinks of Odie less as a person and more like my Disney princess animal companion, which is okay with me. He's my last one so I'm softer with him, happy to let him stay a baby for longer. I'm sucking up every minute of it. I've got no interest in chasing milestones the way I did with the others. I'll probably still be trying to dress him in white linen onesies when he's in high school. But he's better than a Flounder or an Olaf, anyway. He's generous with his giggles and happy to sit and observe the chaotic world going on around him. This might be his nature, his innate personality shining through, or it might be something else, a product of the fact that he has five people in his face all day long, telling him how cute he is, how adorable he is, how loved he is. Who wouldn't grow up to be happy and tolerant and good with that as their entire life experience?

~

People talk about nature versus nurture. I don't know that I believe completely in one or the other. Nature feels too much like the lucky dip where you could end up with the stale Wizz Fizz and nurture relies way too much on my own unqualified abilities. I believe more in circumstance—a little of who you are at birth mixed with other things that make a difference to your experience of the world: your birth order, your relationship with your siblings, the life stage of your parents. 'Siblings grow up in the same house but in totally different worlds' goes the saying. I think it might be true.

THE EXIT STRATEGY

OVER THE LAST decade or so in magazine publishing, all the players had become acutely aware that they may need to consider another career path, and perhaps imminently. A former deputy editor of mine—a suave, debonair man with a wonderfully clever, occasionally filthy, sense of humour and a lifetime of experience on glossies like *Vogue* and *Elle*—used to dream about his next life owning a nail salon. He'd muse on it with a wry grin as we walked out of yet another soul-destroying management meeting where a puffed-up old man in a bad suit had told us that he didn't like our choice of a Cara Delevingne cover—something I usually thought was a good thing given that puffed-up old men in bad suits were generally not our target market—but I'm not sure he was ever really joking.

For me, the alterna-dream was always to be a travel agent, a kind of personalised family concierge where I would get to plan incredible and pathologically detailed holiday itineraries for people who might not have the time or be inclined to do the

research required for such a trip themselves. Personally, I don't understand those people. They're foreign beings to me, like slow walkers and women who claim to love anal sex. I'm the opposite. I sometimes suspect that I get more pleasure from researching a trip than from the actual trip itself.

The joy of planning is never ruined by a carsick child or a meltdown because someone dropped their shaved ice. The armchair travel you do snuggled up with your laptop is never marred by a missed flight or a rainy day or a YouTube-famous magician who cancels the day of the show after you just spent $800 on tickets and rerouted your road trip by sixty kilometres because your twelve-year-old was so desperate to see him. It's not derailed by a goddamn pandemic. The planning runs like clockwork and is always the best time you can ever imagine with your family, mostly because it's not yet tainted by anything that resembles your actual, live family.

In those heady times before the travel industry was brought to its knees, I liked to book my trips as far in advance as possible, which bought me months and months of the joy of anticipation, a light at the end of the tunnel of everyday drudgery. When I was yelling at my kids to get ready and out the door on a Wednesday morning, I was soothed by knowing that one day in the foreseeable scheduled, booked and paid for future, we'd be waking up at a leisurely pace in a foreign city with nothing to think about but whatever adventure I'd meticulously planned for us that day. When I was trying to avoid watching my husband in nothing but his undies giving his groin a lazy scratch in front of *Survivor*, it gave me comfort to know that in just 102 sleeps,

we'd be drinking a bottle of pale rosé in a courtyard covered in bougainvillea, remembering why we fell in love, the greying Calvins merely a distant memory of home.

I could picture all this very clearly, because from the minute we decided to take a trip, I had it all laid out on a spreadsheet that included addresses, reservation codes, prepaid ticket reference numbers, the number of minutes it would take us to get from A to B via Uber or on six-year-old feet, including allocated toilet breaks and locals tips for skipping the queue and what to order from the menu. This from a woman who's made a point of never knowing how to use the printer in any office she's worked in since 2008. But it seems that when it comes to documenting the vital details of three holiday meals and two stops for gelato a day, suddenly my ability to Excel appears as if from nowhere.

If you're one of those people who likes to think of themselves as spontaneous, you're probably reading this and deciding that I am possibly not the most fun person to travel with. But that's where you'd be wrong! Spontaneity is a wonderful thing in many situations—mid-week mental health spa days, living room dance floors halfway through a dinner party—but travel isn't one of them. It costs you more, for one, which means you can do it less. And far from being free to stumble upon some incredible secret lunch spot or cultural activity, you're actually just stuck with the places you can get into, which means they're not that busy, which means they're probably not that good. Like Charlie Chaplin, who famously didn't want to be part of any club that wanted him as a member, I'm not interested in going anywhere that can accept my reservation for six too easily.

Not to say that I'm not flexible if something better pops up or plans change—the mild twitching does stop eventually—but at least I'm out there in the world secure in the knowledge that I'll never be found eating a random mediocre meal in—for example—Austin, Texas, because I didn't realise that Franklin Barbecue, the world's best barbecue, was just around the corner. Or worse, excitedly arriving at Franklin Barbecue at lunchtime only to find out that people start lining up at 8 am, happily standing in line for six hours every day of the week for brisket. Not for free diamonds, for *brisket*. The less savvy traveller would miss out, never to know what can possibly be so good about this food that people send interns to wait all morning in a line for their lunch. That's not spontaneity, that's a tragedy. A bit of prior research, though, would reveal that Franklin offers just a couple of slots a day of takeout, to be ordered six weeks in advance, with a minimum order of five pounds of meat. A methodical traveller (i.e. me) would mark the date in their calendar, set an alarm, wake up in the middle of the night and manage to book a slot. They'd pick up that full five pounds of heart attack and eat it straight from the paper it's wrapped in at a local brewery, having one of the most memorable, most delicious meals of their lives, even though their cholesterol levels might never recover from it. The point being that the world is much too full of wonderful meals to ever waste one because you're free and easy and want to see where the wind takes you. I know where it takes you. It takes you to McDonald's.

~

All of this is why I'm an excellent travel companion, maybe the greatest one ever in fact, because I will joyfully do all the work required to ensure that wasted meals or moments are not an issue that we will ever have to face and I'll do it with a gusto the likes of which you've never seen before. One of my girlfriends, who is probably one of the most efficient and clever women I know, says that she loves travelling with me because while I take on the grunt work of doing all the research and preplanning, she can allow herself to really switch off and travel like a person who doesn't have to think about a thing. When she travels with me, she travels just like Mariah Carey on a global tour, being gently shepherded from place to place with no idea where she's meant to be at any given moment. Which is to say that when she travels with me, she travels like a husband.

It's not just that I love to control every aspect of other people's lives, although there is that. I do actually have the air-mile chops to make my move into the travel industry a credible venture, should the need arise. Before Covid-19 ruined it for everybody, my Qantas app informed me that I'd been flying an average of the equivalent of six times around the world every year. Which implies that I was some fabulous gypset nomad who was never home, but like many parents who have to travel for work, I had the in-and-out business trip down to a fine art:

> 6 am: Wake up, start mentally packing an ordered, perfectly planned capsule wardrobe of only the exact outfits I'm going to wear into a bag small enough to take as carry-on.

6.10 am: Be told the class cake stall is today and that we were nominated to bring the cupcakes. Argue that this is the first time I've heard of this. Find the note scrunched up and banana-stained in the bottom of a schoolbag. 'Homemade preferred!' Give in, because I know that if I don't, my husband may end up sending in a six-pack of Baker's Delight cheese and bacon rolls to the cake stall and I'd be able to feel the parental judgement from the other side of the world. Bake cupcakes. Key ingredients: flour, sugar, panic, resentment.

7.15 am: Give up on the idea of perfect packing and shove anything I find lying on the floor and a few things from the laundry basket into a giant suitcase in the hope that among it all are three event- and weather-appropriate outfits. Race to the airport.

8 am: Just make it to check-in in time. Wait for the flight and start to sweat thinking of everything I didn't do to keep life functioning in my absence. Feel guilty.

9 am: Take my seat on the plane. Call husband and yell 'It's mufti day!' down the phone as the plane takes off, hoping he heard me before all the bars disappeared. Realise afterwards that I didn't specify for which child.

9.01 am: Sit on a plane for twenty-four hours. Fret with guilt and anxiety for the first twenty-one. Revel in the serenity for the last three. Land too soon.

6 pm: Arrive somewhere. Make my way to the hotel.

7 pm: Pack on enough make-up to make myself appear human even though I am literally the walking dead.

7.30 pm: Attend the event I flew halfway around the world for. Talk a lot of rubbish, mostly about how long the flight from Australia is and

how, bizarrely and incredibly, it's winter here now but summer back in Australia. Huzzah, basic geography!

11 pm: Go back to the hotel and go to sleep. No small feet kick me in the kidneys. No-one cries out my name because they've wet the bed. No-one tries to throw a leg over. Enjoy the most restful four hours I've had in weeks.

3 am: Wake up with jet lag and make the mistake of looking at my phone. Do a full eight hours of emails from bed.

11 am: Check out of hotel. Spend three hours running around the city madly trying to find presents to alleviate the guilt for being away. Realise I've just spent more on the presents than I earn for doing the job that has taken me away in the first place. Battle with my life choices.

2 pm: Go to the airport, fly twenty-four hours home, crying the whole way because of a cocktail of altitude, red wine, exhaustion, mediocre rom-coms and more guilt. Feel excited to soon be back in the loving bosom of my family. I just love them so much.

8 am: Land in Sydney. Resent that my husband didn't surprise me with an airport pick-up even though I'd insisted it wasn't necessary because work is paying for a car.

9 am: Get home. Hug my husband and children like I'll never let them go.

9.07 am: Bark at my children for fighting over the gifts I have brought them. Get annoyed that my husband didn't do any laundry while I was gone. Realise that life goes on exactly the same without me and taking one extra day to catch my breath wouldn't have been noticed, let alone scar any of them for life.

9.09 am: Get a call about a work trip to Perth the next week. Ask if I can get in and out in a day. Repeat.

This sort of condensed trip might not sound like a good time and definitely isn't, but it does make you a highly efficient traveller and has some real advantages. Mostly, minimal jet lag once you're back home. If you don't sleep at all on a mini-trip, your body clock will never need to catch up. It's not so good for the bags under your eyes or the general deterioration of your body and spirit, but what do those things matter when you have deadlines to make!

If you do have any free time, I've learned that it's quite possible to get the vibe of a city in a single afternoon, especially when you're not dragging a kindergartener behind you who needs to do yet another wee. When you're used to making your way through the world with a child, the times you don't have one feel like time has slowed, and you can pack twice, no, *ten times* as much activity into any given hour than normal. Or you can just stay in bed and do nothing if you want. Either way, you'll never feel more free.

In general, people who moan about having to travel for work are exaggerating. I know, because I was one of them. I used to whinge about it all the time! Not all my complaints were exaggerated. Of course it's hard to be away from your family. Even harder is all the organisation you have to do before you leave. It's not fun to sit on a plane in the minutes before take-off, ignoring the death stares from the flight attendant as you frantically try to find a last-minute babysitter because the one you'd organised for school pick-up that day has chosen the exact moment you're boarding a thirteen-hour flight to tell you she's sick that day. Or to try to desperately speed-write a speech themed 'If I Were a

Superhero' for the Year 1 public speaking competition in iMessage as your flight is taxiing because it hasn't been done and it's happening *today*.

When any working parent complains about how travelling for work isn't fun and games, how you still have to do all the work you would have done in the office and manage things at home from the other side of the world, how tiring and lonely it can be, they're telling the truth. But the secret, lesser-known truth of it is that once you're in the air and there's nothing you can do about any of it, there's a feeling of liberty that comes over you that you probably haven't experienced since you first realised you were going to have a child—and that in itself is worth all the chaos. Just being alone for the length of a long-haul flight is a special treat when you come from a world where being mid-shit is not enough to stop someone from coming in the room to tell you what they dreamt last night.

Even at the peak of my life as a frequent flyer point-amassing global fashion nomad, when I was so blasé about another trip to Paris or Los Angeles that more than once I showed up on the other side of the world without any make-up or any spare undies like I'd thought I was just popping off to the corner store, there were some things I never took for granted—and flying without small children in tow was one of them. Going somewhere new and exotic with my family is my most favourite thing to do ever, but when you have very young children, the getting there is akin to being stuck for hours in an enclosed space in enemy territory with a ticking time bomb that you will never have enough snacks or baby wipes to diffuse. Luckily, once your kids are older, being

on a plane means that all your internal conflict about screen time goes out the window and everyone is happy to boldly embrace sixteen hours straight of the Marvel Universe. The scars from those early years never fade though, and even when flying squished up against a loud mouth-breather in a teeny tiny economy seat, as long as you don't have your children with you, you will forever feel like you're on the Concorde.

~

The part I always secretly love the most about travelling for work are the airport connections. I got heady on the romance of those big hub airports like Hong Kong or Dubai, with everyone coming and going from all across the world, global citizens of a weirdly timeless bubble filled with endless Longchamp bags and HSBC ads designed to make the sleep-deprived tear up. I loved how mysterious I felt in those places—no-one's mum or wife or employee or daughter, but a person who could be going anywhere, to do anything. I could be so much more interesting than I really was, doing much more interesting things. I could be a scientist off to present my latest work at an international conference where people would talk about how I was a shoo-in for the Nobel, a start-up founder about to kick off a game-changing round of VC funding, a lonely philanthropist about to pick up the child I've adopted from a developing country. I could be *younger*, especially if you only see me from the back.

At those midway points—on a long trip, exhausted by my life on both sides, I'd often find myself staring up at the departures board watching flights to Casablanca or Rio de Janeiro

being called—places I'd never been and might never go—and be in awe of the fact that I am an adult, free to make my own choices, with a passport and a credit card that's not always all the way maxed out in my wallet, and if I really wanted to, I could get myself a ticket and be in one of those places by dinnertime. Casablanca by dinnertime! What a possibility.

But instead I'd choose to come home, to babysitter dramas and speech day fails, to management meetings and endless kid dream recounts. I'd come home but the second I could, I'd settle down with my laptop to plan our next family trip, where I won't be mysterious or interesting to anyone who sees me in transit, but just another bedraggled mother exactly my age, dragging my husband and kids through the airport on an itinerary that doesn't allow for unscheduled toilet breaks. And I wouldn't have it any other way.

Epilogue

COMPLETE BUT NOT FINISHED

LIKE A CAT, I've lived nine lives. Actually, it's probably more and I'd be a fool to assume that's even the final number. One of the only things I know to be absolutely true in this life is that everything is temporary. Anyone who had one of those fringes that you teased into a bird's nest using the palm of your hand and a ten-second-straight stream of Elnett knows that that's a good thing. But it's also why tattoos are problematic, and sometimes marriages.

Joan Didion wrote that she had already lost touch with a couple of people she used to be. Sadly, I've not only lost touch with but have completely forgotten most of mine. They've faded from my brain, like high school trigonometry and the words to Debbie Gibson songs. This sometimes makes me regret that I haven't been the kind of person who was committed enough to keep a journal throughout the more interesting times of my life,

but then I'll find a lone non-starter of a diary entry in an other-wise empty notebook, or pick up an old, melodrama-infused letter I wrote to someone years ago and I'm so relieved that I never had the follow-through. Sometimes I could die of morti-fication just reading the caption on a two-year-old Instagram post. Some versions of you and your choice in filters are best left unremembered.

Most of my personas have been born out of my romantic relationships, which used to embarrass me. Surely it had to be anti-feminist how much history showed that my wardrobe, interests and sometimes even my opinions evolved constantly to match those of whoever I thought I was in love with at any particular time? Now I know there's no way to avoid being influ-enced in that way when you're still really working out who you are. You're only human, not Michelle Obama. Plus, I think I've left most of my boyfriends in a better state sartorially speaking than I found them, so at least it's been an equal opportunity kind of morphing.

Over the years, I've been a Surfer Chick and a Russian Mafia Moll (not the dangerous kind, just a Bondi version), I've lived out all my *Almost Famous* fantasies on tour with a musician and his band, bored myself to distraction playing Corporate Wife across dinner tables with guys who were pushing forty and still asked new people they met where they went to high school, and I had my English soccer WAG days, where my metamorphosis also included picking up a strong London accent that Hayden and the boys once heard in a home VHS tape and rejoice in teasing me about relentlessly to this day. I don't think any of these were

completely false personalities—they were more like tiny little latent parts of me (some more tiny than others) that for a brief period I pretended were the whole.

Even within relationships, we take on different parts that can change over time. We often start out as the Cool Girl, chill and easygoing. You take ex-girlfriends and boys' nights in your stride. You go with him to never-ending footy games and do shots in the pub with his mates afterwards. You're fun! You fit in! You're a keeper! It's of course almost guaranteed that at some point in the future, Cool Girl will become a Nag, shooting dark daggers when he walks in the door late, having dared to go to the gym after work when you've been home with a baby all day. It's a scarily swift progression.

Or maybe once upon a time you're the Sex Kitten, getting ready to see him like you're preparing for war, spending a small fortune on waxing and facials and blow-dries and spray tans and pedicures, slathering yourself in coconut body butter and delicate, expensive hair oils, and applying make-up that took fourteen products and three YouTube tutorials to make you look like you're not wearing any so he thinks this aesthetically and sensorially pleasing-to-the-last-centimetre version of you is how you are naturally, straight out of the box. And suddenly it's eight years and two babies later and you literally could not care less when he walks in on you while you're doing a poo. It's going to happen. Life moves, relationships change, people evolve.

These shifting roles happen in your career too. For the longest time, I was the wunderkind at work, the youngest in the room, the single advantage of never having gone to uni. I can't tell

you the exact moment when that version of me was no longer, but at some point I looked around and found myself a bona fide elder statesman. Often in a meeting it will hit me that I could be the mother of everyone I work with. And I don't mean that as an exaggeration, I mean that I was sexually active the year they were born. I could have literally birthed all my colleagues.

~

Lots of people seem to think that we become a different person every seven years. Philosopher Rudolf Steiner believed in a theory of human development based on seven-year cycles. Astrologists subscribe to continual seven-month growth phases relating to the twelve signs of the zodiac, with a complete cycle, or lesson, taking seven years. There's even a theory that every cell in our bodies is completely regenerated over that time span, which would make us, essentially, a whole new us every seven years.

My own life at the applicable ages does seem to correspond neatly with some fairly super-significant life shifts. Admittedly, I'm highly susceptible to finding truth in this kind of thing. Not that I believe in astrology, but I am *such* a Cancerian.

When I was aged seven, we moved to the suburbs, a place that would redefine how I saw myself, and would have reverberations for years to come. At fourteen, I discovered boys and magazines— and it was pretty much just all boys and magazines for the next seven years. (It's still all boys and magazines to this day, actually, except now the boys are those I've given birth to rather than ones I met at the Caringbah under-18s nightclub, Munchkins.) At twenty-one, I landed in Portugal from London which ended

up bringing my misguided footballer's wife phase to an end in favour of the next full cycle, the freedom years, a time when I considered six tempura oysters and three Kir Royales a night a complete and life-sustaining diet. At twenty-eight, I became a mother, then quickly did it again. At thirty-five, I got married, something that went as well as can be expected when you make a life-altering decision of the heart based on sensible criteria like 'would never cheat on me' and 'my nanna loves him'.

And suddenly I found myself in my forty-second year—the start of my most recent seven-year cycle—getting married to the great love of my life, pregnant with a new baby and about to start a brand-new job. *My cells made me do it.*

Of course, it's not altogether true that all our cells regenerate every seven years. Some special cells in our bodies are with us from birth to death: the inner lens cells of the eye, the neurones in our cerebral cortex—which is the part of the brain that makes us human, determining personality and intelligence as well as thinking and perception—and the muscle cells of the heart. Our eyes, our brain and our hearts: the parts of us where we carry the wisdom of age, the memories of who we once were and the clarity of who we've become.

ACKNOWLEDGEMENTS

I TRIED TO get out of writing this book many times. I tried resisting and back-pedalling. I tried making excuses and pleading my case. I tried to just not write it at all. Many of these times I was pulled back in by Claire Kingston, whose idea this excessively long editor's letter was in the first place. Thank you, Claire. Sorry I was such a pain in the arse. And thanks to Kelly Fagan, Courtney Lick and everyone else at Allen & Unwin for helping to massage this book into existence, however reluctantly it happened. Special love to CT for spending her sleeping hours hunting down that perfect Pantone pink for her cover design, and to Georges Antoni for taking the only pictures of my head that don't plunge me into an existential crisis.

In the times when I did actually write, it resulted in me being a truly crappy and irritable wife and mother. I couldn't be more

grateful to my husband and children for sticking with me despite this. I'll be fun again one day soon, promise.

Thank you to all the friends, Munch and non-Munch, who were constantly asking about and encouraging the writing process even when they knew it would only result in complaining and lamentations, and especially to my ideal readers, Zoë and Bron, for being the very best word cheerleaders a girl could ask for.

A million thank yous to my mum for all that relentless uncon-ditional love, even when I was a real shit of a teen and still now that I'm a self-focused grown-up who calls on you to help raise my own children way more often than is proper. I hope the maternal pride you feel in being able to tell your friends that your daughter wrote a book isn't negated by the fact that they all now know more about my sex life than you could surely ever want them to. And to my Nanna and Pa, the greatest love story I ever knew and only inspiration I've ever needed. I miss you both every day.

To the girls who feel somehow less-than and to the women who feel so fucking tired, I feel you.

And, finally, to Fromager D'Affinois: when times are tough you always come through for me. Thank you for being you.